MAKING
MONEY
MORAL

JUDITH RODIN AND SAADIA MADSBJERG

MAKING MONEY MORAL

HOW A NEW WAVE OF VISIONARIES IS LINKING PURPOSE *AND* PROFIT

WHARTON
SCHOOL
PRESS
Philadelphia

Published by Wharton School Press
The Wharton School
University of Pennsylvania
3620 Locust Walk
300 Steinberg Hall-Dietrich Hall
Philadelphia, PA 19104
Email: whartonschoolpress@wharton.upenn.edu
Website: wsp.wharton.upenn.edu

Ebook ISBN: 978-1-61363-109-6
Paperback ISBN: 978-1-61363-110-2

For our children and the future we want for them

Contents

Introduction

On land, turtles move slowly. Yet once in the ocean, they glide with grace, their cumbersome forms liberated from gravity, the sun-dappled water turning their shells into miraculous multicolored artworks. But turtles are not the only creatures the oceans bring to life. Oceans also sustain millions of human lives. This is particularly true for the Seychelles, an archipelago in the Indian Ocean that is home to five of the world's seven remaining turtle species. Whether raising families or engaged in fishing or tourism, the citizens of this island nation depend almost entirely on the waters surrounding them for their health, nutrition, and livelihoods.

Few people understand this better than Angelique Pouponneau. She is CEO of the Seychelles Conservation and Climate Adaptation Trust (SeyCCAT), a public-private trust that supports ocean initiatives, especially those benefiting women. And she knows that ocean degradation, whether from overfishing or from the effects of climate change on marine ecosystems, not only has consequences for nature—it also has an immediate impact on local families. "It's ocean health for human health," she said. "And it's livelihoods and food security as a whole."[1]

Pouponneau cites the example of a local fisher's wife, who relies on fish to feed her family and sells her husband's catch at the local market or by the side of the road. "She's a mother, and the most nutritional source of protein is fish from the lovely waters of the Seychelles," she said. If ocean degradation means her husband starts bringing in less catch, the family may still have enough to eat. However, their livelihood depends on what the fisher's wife can sell.

Real communities. Real people. Real lives. These are not often associated with the world of high finance. But they can often play a critical role. To protect the oceans so vital to these communities, in 2018 the government of Seychelles created a highly innovative financial instrument designed to raise funding that, by supporting sustainable marine and fisheries projects, could preserve and improve the livelihoods of its citizens. It was a global first: a sovereign blue bond. With the World Bank Treasury helping to develop the bond and three key investors—Calvert Impact Capital, Nuveen (a subsidiary of TIAA), and Prudential Financial—the bond raised $15 million.

With the $500,000 that SeyCCAT receives every year from the blue bond, it has funded 17 projects, ranging from initiatives that strengthen ocean ecosystem protection to those that support sustainable marine enterprises. Some do both. For example, a project to establish a monitoring protocol for the parrotfish sector will help government fishery management agencies and researchers develop improved techniques for managing parrotfish stocks. Parrotfish are essential to the maintenance of healthy, resilient coral reefs. Because they excrete hundreds of pounds of the white sand annually, they are also vital to the attractiveness of Seychelles as a tourist destination. The project will therefore benefit both artisanal fisheries and tourism businesses while also ensuring healthy stocks of parrotfish and the preservation of coral reefs.

The Seychelles's life-protecting blue bond is an example of what can happen when the world of capital markets meets the world of impact—or, as we argue in the title of this book, when we work to make money moral. It builds on a growing market for social and green bonds backed by investors wanting financial products that generate positive social or environmental impact, as well as financial returns. The blue bond soon inspired comparable products on a much larger scale, such as the SEK (Swedish krona) 2 billion (about $215 million), five-year Nordic Investment Bank's Nordic–Baltic Blue Bond, focused on water resource management and protection. It is part of a flowering of innovation and an explosion of new tools that enable private capital to address everything from poverty to carbon emissions while generating competitive financial returns for investors.

The growing momentum behind this idea comes as the unfettered pursuit of profit and the mantra of "shareholder primacy" are being increasingly challenged. Traditionally, investors gave little to no importance to social and environmental issues when making investment decisions. The ideology was to separate the creation of wealth from the distribution of wealth. The moral side happened at the distributional level and was the responsibility of government and nonprofits.

But this is changing. Today, it is becoming increasingly clear to policymakers, investors, and business leaders that neither business nor financial markets can outrun the impact of social and environmental issues, and that profit and purpose are strongly linked. The focus is shifting to strategies that both exclude potentially catastrophic environmental, social, and governance risks from investment portfolios and include more investments that drive long-term growth and value for investors *and* society. These strategies will "make money moral" and contribute to a more equitable and sustainable world.

And now, as the world has confronted its greatest challenge in a generation—the COVID-19 pandemic—everything we have taken for granted has come into question, from employment and children's education to public health systems. How, in this new world, should financial resources be used to rebuild and sustain communities, workers, and livelihoods? What role should capital markets play in preserving natural resources and battling the next great global crisis: climate change?

Of course, beginning in early 2020, the investment community embarked on something of a roller-coaster ride as a result of the uncertainties prompted by COVID-19. What also emerged during the crisis was a recognition that going back to business as usual was no longer an option.

However, we believe the changes that will arise could be built on the strong foundation laid over the past few decades, which has seen the emergence of the powerful new financial strategy of linking purpose and profit. We call it "sustainable and impact investing," and it has the capacity to transform capitalism. As we will show in this book, it's an idea that has caught fire.

When Money Managers Meet Problem Solvers

This transformation will take more than finance. It will take collaboration. And the Seychelles's blue bond is a good illustration of how this happens. The bond's development and its subsequent management brought together a national finance institution and an international finance institution, large global investors, international donors, and a conservation organization. As the blue bond demonstrates, sustainable and impact investing cannot be driven by one organization or sector alone. A number of different actors each play a part.

First, there are those in legal possession of the capital, the asset owners (from individuals to large pension funds, insurance companies, and sovereign wealth funds). They decide how and where to allocate funds, according to their objectives and current market conditions. And in recent years, social and environmental considerations have been playing an increasingly prominent part in those decisions, with many allocating more of their portfolios to sustainable and impact investing.

Enabling their objectives to be realized are two key groups: the money managers and the problem solvers. In sustainable and impact investing, the financial resources and expertise of the money managers are what enable large-scale capital flows to be directed toward solving global challenges—social and environmental issues that the problem solvers are working to fix. So who belongs to each of these two groups? We define money managers as the asset managers and intermediaries—from fund managers and investment consultants to the sustainable investment offices of large banks—who need to satisfy clients' growing demand for sustainable and impact investing products and funds. In the process, they are amassing significant experience in building impact portfolios. In every asset class, they are developing financial mechanisms that can attract new sources of capital or bring together different types of capital in new ways. They are developing tools that assess social and environmental impact early in the investment decision-making process (origination and due diligence), and that ensure investments are indeed having the intended impact.

We define the problem solvers as an even wider group. They are the government agencies, advocacy groups, and large nongovernmental organizations (NGOs) working to solve everything from poverty and infant mortality to pollution, water scarcity, and climate change. They are the entrepreneurs looking for the capital with which to create and scale businesses that can solve some of these problems. They are philanthropies and NGOs that want to harness new sources of capital or engage in partnerships that will enable them to have greater impact. And they are public companies that are developing clean, green, and sustainable products, services, and business models, often in response to pressure from investors to address the negative and demonstrate the positive impacts of their businesses. In the sustainable and impact investing sphere, problem solvers play two key roles: They can tap directly into new sources of investment capital, and, by bringing expertise to the table and convening governments, companies, and investors, they dramatically impact the field as a whole.

As these two communities join forces, exciting collaborations are emerging between sectors, each using unique skills and resources in new ways to pursue investments and increase funding flows. This can dramatically increase the scale and accelerate the speed at which solutions can be found to many of the world's problems. When these two communities come together, things get really interesting.

A Broad Spectrum of Investors and Tools

Sustainable and impact investors array along a broad spectrum. At one end are those evaluating their portfolios through an ESG (environmental, social, and governance) lens, selecting existing companies that are working to improve their social and environmental footprints. From these companies, investors demand action and disclosure on everything from gender equity and human rights to climate change, deforestation, and water security. At the other end of the spectrum are impact investors. They are not investing in companies simply to reduce their negative impacts. They are providing capital to create or grow entirely new types of companies and programs—ones established with the explicit purpose of solving a social or environmental problem or delivering a sustainable service while also generating financial returns.

Investors build sustainable and investment programs in different ways, with different return outcomes. For a small number, building a portfolio means signaling their values rather than looking to outperform. For an increasing number, however, it is a source of investment value—a strategy for managing risk and generating alpha.

Some advocates argue that the "sustainable and impact investing" category should include negative screening—eliminating so-called sin stocks such as tobacco or guns from a portfolio—and divestment from fossil fuels. These are among the oldest, best-known strategies, and there are valid reasons for pursuing them. However, we believe far more can be accomplished by allocating investment dollars to strategies that provide financing for positive solutions to these problems.

Investors now have a wide choice of entry points in both public and private markets. Let's say an investor wants to focus on gender diversity and on improving life for women and girls. One option would be a gender-based exchange-traded fund that invests in large global public companies promoting workforce gender diversity. Another might be to use a gender lens in evaluating angel investments. Private equity also offers opportunities through investments in companies that are developing products and services for women and girls (for example, health products in mature markets or cook stoves in developing countries). And asset managers can use gender as one of their impact themes in fixed-income portfolios.

Growing Investments—with Room for Growth

As the number of investment options increases, so does the number of investors putting their money where their mouth is. By the start of 2018, in the United States alone, assets under management (AUM) using sustainable strategies stood at $12 trillion—$1 of every $4. Across the five major world markets, the total figure was almost $31 trillion.[2]

That might sound large. However, $31 trillion is still only around one-third of the discretionary AUM of the world's 500 largest asset managers, which in 2018 stood at roughly $92 trillion. When it comes to sustainable and impact investing, the numbers are getting bigger—but there's still some way to go.

Of course, we are not suggesting that the private sector should or will become the only source of funding through which to address social and environmental challenges. While we will not be covering these sources, public financing raised through taxation and financing with longer time horizons or lower (concessional) returns in exchange for higher impact remains critical. Nor are we suggesting that "financial-only" investments are inappropriate—in many cases they are and will continue to be for many investors.

However, it is now becoming clear that financial innovations, when combined with private-sector dollars, can make essential contributions to fixing big global problems. This takes the pressure off charitable funding, strategic grant making, and catalytic and development capital so that more of these dollars can be directed toward causes that lack business model solutions and will never attract commercial investors.

For Better and Worse

For sustainable and impact investments to continue to attract mainstream investors, their financial performance is critical. And over the past few years, funds using ESG in their investment process have performed well. Morgan Stanley research on the performance of almost 11,000 mutual funds between 2004 and 2018 showed no financial trade-off between the returns of sustainable funds (which also came with lower downside risk) and those of traditional funds. In *Bloomberg*'s fourth-annual ranking of ESG mutual funds—those with five-year track records and at least $100 million in assets—nine were outperforming the market in 2019, while seven of the funds outperformed over the past five years.[3] The same is true for impact funds. Respondents to the 2019 Annual Impact Investor Survey from the Global Impact Investing Network (GIIN) indicated that portfolio performance—in emerging and developed markets as well as the market as a whole—had met or exceeded their expectations for both social and environmental impact and financial return.[4]

This, however, was before 2020, when COVID-19 turned the world on its head. As the catastrophic social and economic consequences of the pandemic became apparent, a question arose: Would the push toward linking purpose and profit be swept aside in the chaos? Yet, like other defense-oriented strategies, sustainable and impact investing can reduce volatility since sustainable business practices focus on things like building resilient supply chains, managing environmental risks, and cutting fossil fuel energy use—all of which help companies survive economic and market turbulence. COVID-19 would be the greatest test yet of this principle.

In the first months of 2020, mounting evidence suggested that ESG strategies were in fact holding their ground. "Sustainable funds have performed well relative to conventional funds amid the global pandemic," wrote Jon Hale, head of sustainability research for Morningstar, in a post on June 24, noting that ESG funds had been setting a record pace for launches in 2020. "They have also received record levels of flows. The pandemic and the movement for racial justice in the United States have likely increased investor interest and will prompt even more people to follow through on that interest with actual investments."[5]

In fact, by June 2020—several months into the pandemic—market and investor signals seemed to indicate that sustainable and impact investing approaches were being seen as a way to not only weather economic storms but also create portfolios that could out-perform the market. Of course, the data may change yet again, as may the analysis of why these approaches are delivering both impact and financial returns. However, indications so far are that these two goals are not, as was once thought, mutually exclusive. The pandemic is not the first crisis, nor will it be the last, for which this will be the case. But for many, the pandemic has been a loud wake-up call that our economic system is on shaky foundations, built on hyper-leveraged, unfettered growth, without regard for nature and not built for resilience. In an uncertain world, sustainable and impact investing approaches offer a means of building resilience into investment portfolios while also contributing to a better world.

Why We Wrote This Book

We aim to explain, evaluate, and help accelerate the growth of this dynamic new market for making money moral. We will describe how it works with real-life examples, identify the key players, showcase the most promising innovations, and highlight the greatest opportunities both for investors and for people and the planet. We will explore some of the innovative products and investment strategies that money managers—often in collaboration with problem solvers—have been developing to meet the growing appetite for sustainable and impact investing. And we will reflect on how these approaches are helping improve lives and protect ecosystems and natural resources.

We come to this as funders, investors, authors, speakers, and conveners, who have been deeply involved in accelerating the development of the sustainable and impact investing field globally. Over the years, we've built relationships with countless members of the sustainable and impact investing community—asset owners, money managers, problem solvers, and others. The views of many of them appear in this book, for which we have conducted extensive interviews. We have talked to experts and innovators working on the cutting edge of sustainable and impact investing. Their knowledge and insights have helped us shape the pages that follow.

Our senior roles at The Rockefeller Foundation gave us the resources and the global platform needed to work at the intersection of sustainable development and capital markets. We funded a considerable array of pilot work leading to innovation in finance, and then invested and worked with others to take successful ideas to scale.

It's been quite a journey. It started in 2007, when The Rockefeller Foundation convened a group of investors, entrepreneurs, and philanthropists at its Bellagio Conference Center in Italy, at which the term "impact investing" was coined. Back then, while the time was ripe for sustainable and impact investing, the supply side—the capital—was poorly organized, moving too cautiously, and lacking in leadership.

We spent the next decade building out the critical elements needed to accelerate the deployment of capital to double-bottom-line outcomes: platforms, research, metrics, suggested regulatory frameworks, and pilots expanding sustainable and impact investing to new types of asset classes, such as insurance. We helped the field mature and saw new products and strategies emerge in every asset class, laying the groundwork for large-scale investment and growth models that take a longer-term view of environmental protection and social inclusion, and that adopt a broader purpose. And today, we are witnessing the fruits of this early work: the unleashing of vast resources that are generating value for the investors while delivering a positive impact to the planet and the lives it supports.

However, we also understand the danger in rushing to develop transformative financial instruments: If these instruments are unable to preserve impact integrity, we risk diluting the gains we have made. We are therefore also writing this book to share what we have learned to help guide more robust future growth.

Meanwhile, over the years we've come to know many problem solvers who are eager to engage with capital markets but lack the necessary tools—and few resources are available to help people understand and assess the opportunities and their implications. We want to help fill this gap.

The impact economy will take time to evolve fully. But the pace of change has accelerated dramatically in the past decade. Today, significant energy and intellectual forces are being directed toward developing these new mechanisms. We want to highlight some of the exciting innovations we are seeing in sustainable and impact investing—those already available to investors and those at earlier stages of development but that could fuel the next wave of innovation.

In the first five chapters, we will examine how the impact and sustainable investment agenda has matured into a new form of capitalism, explore many different types of investment strategies that can link purpose and profit, and explain how to measure different forms of impact. In chapters 6, 7, and 8, we'll introduce you to the multiple players in this new form of capitalism—the money managers and the problem solvers. In chapter 9 and the epilogue, we will look at what's ahead for this movement.

This book has a further purpose. For what was perhaps most exciting about our work at the foundation was playing the role of broker—sitting at a table with an asset manager on one side and the head of an environmental or development organization on the other, both passionate about contributing to the creation of a better form of capitalism. It's this process that we want to continue through this book, helping money managers and problem solvers learn more about each other and about how, through productive partnership, they can advance a form of investment that benefits both the environment and every segment of society.

We have seen firsthand how sustainable and impact investing can change lives. In the next chapter, we'll look at how, in recent decades, many business leaders started to revise their priorities and adopt more responsible, sustainable approaches to making money. Meanwhile, a growing number of investors took a similar approach and started thinking about how their capital could play a bigger role in securing a more sustainable economy. Now, as capitalism comes under greater scrutiny and the financial sector starts to look ahead at its role in recovery from the COVID-19 crisis, we believe that making money moral is essential for the next chapter in its evolution.

PART I

The Market

Chapter 1

Capitalism Changes Course

During his time working at a traditional financial advisory firm, David MacDonald spent many hours soul-searching. And as he thought about how his industry was shaping the fate of the planet and the life that depends on it, he came to a conclusion: The biggest impact he could have as an individual would be to turn his own industry on its head by creating a firm focused on the environment, one that would help clients understand how their money could be put to work for the good of the environment and communities. This is the goal of The Path, the ethical financial advisory firm he launched in 2018. "I've spent my whole career trying to get people more engaged with their pension," said MacDonald.[6] "And, let's face it, pensions are complex and boring, and as a consequence engagement is really low. But this impact-oriented approach can give you more purpose around your money and around your life—and when you marry your passion and your purpose, you start to be a force to be reckoned with."

"By lots of little pots of money coming together, individual investors can change the mood music," he said. "And so ultimately, we can change the nature of capitalism."

Linking Purpose and Profit

It is a philosophy that is very different from the idea that has influenced mainstream financial industry thinking since 1970, when economist Milton Friedman wrote in the *New York Times* that "the social responsibility of business is to increase its profits."[7] His approach led political, economic, and intellectual forces to line up behind the idea that the primary purpose of business is to increase earnings and return those earnings to companies' owners: its shareholders. It is an idea known as "shareholder primacy." However, in the past decade it has come under increased scrutiny. In the process, demand has been growing for new sustainable options in everything from clothing and food to financial products. And, more broadly, in public debates and company boardrooms, questions are being asked about the purpose of business, of financial markets, and of capitalism itself.

Part of this has grown out of what's known as "conscious consumerism." From the fair trade movement, which emerged in the 1960s, to the student boycotts of university-logo clothing in the 1990s protesting against sweatshop manufacturing conditions, consumers have been challenging the role of business in society through their spending power and demanding that companies tell them how what they buy is being produced and what is its social and environmental impact.

Activists have also driven changes in attitudes. In the late 1990s, for example, capitalism's detractors took to the streets when the antiglobalization movement set its sights on the World Trade Organization. At a WTO meeting in Seattle in 1999, protests turned violent, with scenes of vandalism and hundreds of arrests broadcast on TV screens across the globe. With the protesters' anger fueled by everything from industrial pollution to the shifting of jobs to countries with low labor costs, the activities of large corporations came under the spotlight. In subsequent years, armed with a powerful new tool—the internet—campaign groups could target big brands and rapidly spread the word about their poor environmental and human rights record to vast audiences.

Recognizing the need to respond to these trends, large companies began embracing what was then known as corporate social responsibility (CSR). Industry groups, such as the World Business Council for Sustainable Development, started emerging to promote more environmentally and socially responsible business practices. However, CSR was often limited to charitable donations or company investments in the communities around their offices or factories. At its worst, CSR involved little more than public relations and a new mission statement.

Colin Mayer, an Oxford University professor, remembers it well. "By the time the [2008–2009] financial crisis had hit, corporate social responsibility had become a buzzword and lots of companies were jumping onto that bandwagon," recalled Mayer, who has long studied the role of the corporation in contemporary society.[8] With CSR operating in a corporate silo—generally seen as a nice-to-have rather than a must-have strategy—it's unsurprising that, in the wake of the banking crisis, these efforts were often abandoned. "Many companies that were actively pursuing CSR policies suddenly jettisoned them," said Mayer. "There was a financial problem and CSR basically went out of the window."

That might have been the end of it. However, savvier companies were beginning to recognize that consumer demands for ethically and responsibly manufactured products were not going away. Nor were the challenges from consumers and activists, with student anti-sweatshop protests continuing in the wake of the financial crisis. Meanwhile, risks created by climate change were rising on the agenda, with the debate extending beyond the domain of international agencies and NGOs to the private sector. In 2009, for example, global reinsurer Swiss Re was an official member at the Copenhagen Climate Summit (COP 15). And when, in 2009, the annual Edelman Trust Barometer showed trust in business falling in many countries and hitting an all-time low in the United States, even some corporate leaders started challenging the mechanisms of capitalism. Among them was Paul Polman, who, upon assuming his post as CEO of Unilever in 2009, announced that the consumer goods company would abandon quarterly earnings reports in favor of a longer-term value-creation model that embraced equitable and sustainable business practices.

Many of the new perspectives were captured in a 2011 *Harvard Business Review* article titled "Creating Shared Value." In the article, Michael Porter, founder of the modern strategy field and one of the world's most influential management thinkers, along with his colleague Mark Kramer, argues that companies could prosper more fully by incorporating social and environmental considerations into their strategies.[9] A year later, Lynn Stout published a book titled *The Shareholder Value Myth: How Putting Shareholders First Harms Investors, Corporations, and the Public*, in which the Cornell Law School professor argues that putting shareholders first by focusing on short-term returns not only causes companies to pursue business strategies that hurt everyone from investors to employees, customers, and communities, but also is not in the best financial interests of companies and their investors.[10]

"Once it moved beyond CSR, a lot of the debate was really about how to succeed in doing well by doing good," Mayer said. "Then by the end of 2019, the notion of putting 'purpose beyond profit,' as some people put it, had become commonplace and was being widely discussed."

Today, the sense of urgency surrounding climate change has reached a new intensity. Many now see climate change and natural resource depletion as global emergencies—bringing even more dire consequences than COVID-19—with the discussion shifting from the notion that we have to act to save the planet to a recognition that we need to save the planet to save ourselves, and that companies are an essential part of both the problem and the solution.

In 2020, the COVID-19 pandemic and the growing focus on human rights and systemic racial disparities also prompted renewed discussions of the role of business in society. With people's lives and livelihoods feeling increasingly uncertain and the pandemic further widening the already severe levels of social and economic inequity, companies were seen as responsible for the health and welfare of their employees and their communities more than ever. If the financial sector was already being pushed to consider broader sets of stakeholders, in the post-pandemic world this pressure will be something no one can afford to ignore.

The Rise of the Conscious Investor

When Liesel Pritzker Simmons, an heir to the wealth of the Pritzker family, started thinking about embarking on impact investing, she immediately ran into an obstacle: her wealth advisors. "They had no idea what to show me," she said.[11] "They thought I didn't know anything about markets or finance and that what I meant when I said I wanted to align my investments with my values was that I wanted to give it all away—and that wasn't what I meant at all." Rather, she was looking for a way to link purpose and profit. As part of that effort, she and Ian Simmons, her husband, cofounded their family office, Blue Haven Initiative, in 2012 with impact investing as its mission.

Her early bet has paid off. "In 2012, there was a lot of skepticism about making business decisions based on your social values. The thinking then was that doing so would necessarily mean giving up profit," she recalled. This, she says, has changed as evidence has emerged that companies with robust strategies for addressing their social and environmental impact can perform as well as, if not better than, others. "And some of them have at least a decade of track record," she said.

In shifting her entire family office portfolio into impact investing, Pritzker Simmons has been something of a pioneer. However, she is not alone in wanting to align her investments with her values. In 2019, research by the Morgan Stanley Institute for Sustainable Investing found that more than 8 in 10 individual American investors were interested in sustainable investing, while half had taken part in at least one sustainable investing activity.[12] And as the next generation—which stands to inherit more than $30 trillion of wealth in the next 30 years—takes over making investment decisions, many are applying an ESG lens to their investments or shifting their investment strategies into impact investing.

As with the rise of conscious consumerism, for many, the impetus behind changing investment approaches has been the sense that capitalism, in its present form, is not working for everyone. A 2019 investor survey conducted by The Rockefeller Foundation and Longitude, a *Financial Times* company, points to one substantial driver of the adoption of impact investing by retail investors: millennial respondents, a generation hit hard by the 2008 crisis, who see impact investing as a tool to fix a financial system that is "inherently imbalanced or unequal."[13]

In some cases, governments have supported such developments. In 2001, France introduced a "90-10" socially responsible employee savings scheme. It requires companies with more than 50 employees to offer them (in addition to regular saving schemes) an optional solidarity-savings fund that allocates 5% to 10% of its assets to eligible (unlisted) social enterprises, with the remaining 90% to 95% invested in classic (listed) companies, mostly following sustainable or impact investing principles.

Building Blocks for a New Investment Movement

Not only did individuals want to change how they invest their money, but so did some of the world's biggest institutional asset owners. In chapter 3, we describe these in detail. However, part of what has enabled them to do so is that a number of nonfinancial actors first stepped in to create the necessary infrastructure.

Philanthropy was one of them. In the early days, foundations funded pilot work, invested in open-source metrics and platforms, and showed pathways to scale. Sometimes, they also provided the first layer of risk capital, brought together stakeholders, and identified new financing models that could be applied to social and environmental problems.

In 2007, for example, we and our colleagues at The Rockefeller Foundation—through grant making and program-related investments—helped build the impact investing field, seeding new instruments, funding the development of widely used metrics such as the Impact Reporting and Investment Standards (IRIS) and the Global Impact Investing Rating System (GIIRS), and engaging with investors.

Subsequently, several foundations started using their endowments to make impact and mission-related investments. In 2012, for example, the Heron Foundation committed to investing 100% of its assets in alignment with its mission of combating poverty. And in 2017, the Ford Foundation made a commitment to direct up to $1 billion from its $12 billion endowment to mission-related investments.

Meanwhile in 2009, the Global Impact Investing Network (GIIN) was created to bring together impact investors and accelerate the sector's development by encouraging the exchange of knowledge and experience, providing tools and resources, and building the evidence base for the industry.

Other sectors played a key role. In 2012, Big Society Capital was established, with Sir Ronald Cohen as its chairman, as a new type of public-private partnership. Using unclaimed assets (funds in dormant bank accounts swept after a time by the UK government), Big Society Capital's purpose was to advance a social investment marketplace in the UK by stimulating the creation of social finance investment intermediaries that would manage funds and create and raise investment for funds that could provide loans or invest equity in social sector organizations. In June 2013, the UK government, then holding the G8 presidency, announced at the G8 Social Impact Investment Forum the launch of the Social Impact Investment Taskforce, whose goal was to spearhead a global impact investing market.

The United Nations has also played a significant role. Its Principles for Responsible Investment (UNPRI)—launched in April 2006 at the New York Stock Exchange with 100 signatories—now has 3,110 signatories, including some of the world's largest investment managers, such as BlackRock, State Street Global Advisors (SSGA), Amundi, and Fidelity. These organizations and others have provided the basis for, and momentum behind, sustainable and impact investing.

With corporate capitalism starting to embrace new sustainability priorities and many in the investment community following suit, the first two decades of the twenty-first century witnessed a

noticeable shift in mood. This prepared the way for another phe-
nomenon: the movement of large sums of investment capital into
sustainable and impact investing. We turn next to how and why the
field is maturing, generating vast new funding streams to solve
some of the world's biggest problems.

Chapter 2

A New Investment Movement Matures

I n 2010, PensionDanmark, one of Europe's 50 largest pension funds with €36 billion ($41 billion) in assets under management (AUM) at the end of 2019, embarked on what at the time may have been seen as an unlikely partnership: a renewable infrastructure joint venture with a large Danish energy company. Plenty of obstacles lay on the path to sustainable and impact investing. In March 2010, for example, a report from a series of global workshops hosted by the United Nations Environment Programme Finance Initiative and the World Business Council for Sustainable Development found that companies and investors still did not agree on which ESG factors were financially material and that gaps persisted in communications on ESG between company sustainability managers and asset managers, who did not speak the same language.[14]

For PensionDanmark, however, the logic of the partnership with Ørsted (then called DONG Energy) was clear. It was the aftermath of the financial crisis and investors were operating in a low-interest-rate environment. The fund was looking for better investment options. "We needed to get access to assets that could provide a more stable return than we could get from equity markets but also a more attractive return than what we could get from traditional bond markets," explained Torben Möger Pedersen, PensionDanmark's CEO.[15] For Ørsted, it was the early days of changing its business model from dirty to clean energy.

Bringing together a large pension fund responsible for providing a financially secure retirement for its more than 752,500 members and an industrial player like Ørsted was not easy. "We spent months in discussions and negotiations to develop a joint venture model," recalled Möger Pedersen. Ørsted went on to transform itself from being one of Europe's most intensive fossil fuel companies to the world's most sustainable company. For PensionDanmark, it was just the beginning of a series of large-scale renewable infrastructure investments.

In 2012, the pension fund became the founding investor in the Copenhagen Infrastructure Partners (CIP), a fund management company that by 2020 had seven funds with around €9.5 billion ($10.7 billion) in AUM, all focused on the regulated infrastructure and renewable energy fields. "In the beginning, we were the only investor, but we have broadened the investor base and we are now more than 50 institutional investor members," recalled Möger Pedersen, adding that CIP has developed into the world's largest green energy infrastructure investment fund. In June 2020, CIP announced the first close of a new fund, Copenhagen Infrastructure IV, which was on track to become the world's largest renewable fund.

CIP is not the only collective sustainability initiative Pension-Danmark has joined. In 2019, it was among a group of Danish pension funds announcing a commitment to allocate 10% of private pension assets to green investments such as offshore wind farms, photovoltaic energy, climate-friendly properties, and energy storage infrastructure.

As PensionDanmark's story demonstrates, individual investors are not alone in wanting to find new ways of deploying their money. Large asset owners such as pension funds, insurance companies, sovereign wealth funds, development finance institutions, and foundation and university endowments are all starting to embrace strategies that go beyond financial returns and seek social and environmental impact, often through the lens of formal ESG metrics.

"The very large-scale asset owners in Europe, and to some degree in the US, are at the forefront of moving through ESG integration and stewardship into active tilting and targeting of portfolios to ESG-related risks and opportunities, and then on into allocating capital directly both for financial return but also for impact purposes," said Rowan Douglas, head of the Capital, Science & Policy Practice at Willis Towers Watson, a leading global advisory.[16]

Several investor groups with considerable financial clout have emerged on the impact stage. In 2019, for example, 477 investors holding $34 trillion in assets (including pension funds, particularly in Europe and Japan) demanded action to meet the goals of the Paris Agreement on climate change. In Europe, a coalition of investors, including those managing more than €550 billion ($618 billion) in Dutch pension assets, has committed to use the United Nations' Sustainable Development Goals (SDGs) as the framework for a growing amount of their investments.

Signals of a Shift in the Zeitgeist Among Money Managers

By late 2019 and early 2020, the changing behavior of money managers—driven by shifting sentiment among the most powerful asset owners—started making headlines. It was a moment when long-held views on the purpose of capitalism were being challenged with unprecedented intensity. Even before COVID-19, the Hong Kong human rights protests, and Black Lives Matter demonstrations transformed the global social and economic landscape, there was a sense that things could not continue at the status quo.

An important signal came in August 2019, when one of America's biggest business groups, the Business Roundtable (BRT), issued a declaration that broke with corporate orthodoxy. The 181 CEOs who signed its Statement on the Purpose of a Corporation committed to running their companies for the benefit of not only customers and shareholders but also employees, suppliers, and the communities in which they work.[17] In the statement, Bill McNabb, former CEO of Vanguard, one of the world's largest fund managers, was quoted as saying: "By taking a broader, more complete view of corporate purpose, boards can focus on creating long-term value, better serving everyone—investors, employees, communities, suppliers and customers."

Soon after, in January 2020, Larry Fink, BlackRock's CEO, wrote in his annual letter that, henceforth, the firm would apply the same analytical rigor to ESG performance as it does to traditional measures such as credit and liquidity risk. When the CEO of BlackRock—the world's largest asset manager, with a staggering $7 trillion in AUM—makes an announcement, people tend to take note.

Also in January, when world leaders, corporate chiefs, and others gathered in Davos, Switzerland, for the World Economic Forum's annual meeting, it was to discuss how a different type of capitalism could benefit all of society's stakeholders. Speeches and panels focused on the risks and opportunities created by climate change and the SDGs—and how business and investors should respond.[18]

Of course, some of these statements should be viewed with a degree of skepticism. The BRT, for instance, lobbied the Securities and Exchange Commission (SEC) to raise the threshold for initial proposal submissions for shareholder resolutions, which will hamper shareholders' ability to push companies to act on issues such as gender diversity or climate change. And while the BRT took early action to form a COVID-19 task force, it did not issue guidance to companies on best practices. Several member companies were called out for failing to support their employees. In BlackRock's case, five months after Fink issued his letter, a growing number of campaigners and members of the European parliament were calling for the European Union, which in April had selected BlackRock to advise on integrating sustainability into its banking regulations, to reverse its decision. Among the grievances was the fact that the firm had voted against or abstained in 82% of climate-related resolutions at companies in which it invests.

Nevertheless, influential money managers and corporate leaders have increasingly felt the need to amplify their view of the purpose of business and investment. And the media have mirrored the shift.

In January 2020, Bloomberg Media launched Bloomberg Green, an editorial platform focused on climate change. Three months earlier, in September 2019, the *Financial Times* launched a new brand campaign that challenged the status quo, choosing this headline for its New Agenda strategy: "Capitalism: Time for a Reset." When one of the world's leading business newspapers calls for a reset in global capitalism, it's clear that change is on the horizon.

Opportunities for Risk Mitigation and Value Creation

Behind the shifts in financing flows are financial drivers that, even before sustainable and impact investing emerged on the scene, were important to fiduciary responsibility: risk mitigation and the pursuit of value-creation opportunities.

On the risk side, it has become increasingly clear that neither business nor financial markets can outrun the costs of social and environmental risks. In a 2006 survey by the CDP (formerly the Carbon Disclosure Project), just 10% of the FTSE 100, the 100 largest companies listed on the London Stock Exchange, said they considered climate change impacts a high risk to their business operations.[19] Fast-forward to 2019, and the UK's Carbon Trust found that two-thirds (67%) of UK companies said they planned to disclose climate-related risks and opportunities in that year's annual reporting.[20]

While much of the focus has been on "black swans" (events or trends that come as a surprise and have a devastating effect, such as the 2008 US housing market crash), increasing attention is being paid to "green swans" (events or trends that are highly obvious and highly probable, but still neglected by policymakers and investors because they seem intangible or remote). COVID-19 has been the first such event, but it's unlikely to be the last. The economic burden of climate change is increasingly heavy, with costs to the United States of hundreds of billions of dollars a year by 2090, according to some estimates, and the Bank of International Settlements predicting that climate change could trigger another global financial crisis.

On the opportunity side, investors increasingly began to recognize that they could receive attractive financial yields by investing in sustainable businesses and programs. According to the Global Commission on the Economy and Climate, accelerating climate action could by 2030 generate direct economic gains of $26 trillion compared with a business-as-usual approach.[21] The opportunities extend to challenges such as inequality. For example, the World Economic Forum estimates China could gain an additional $1 trillion in GDP growth by 2030 if it solved social inequality over the next decade, while the United States could gain $866.7 billion from doing so.[22]

For investors in public equities, the rewards of a different focus are becoming more apparent as well. According to the third-annual *Barron's* ranking of America's Most Sustainable Companies, shares in the 100 companies on the list generated average returns of 34.3% in 2019, beating the S&P 500 index, whose average was 31.5%. More than half (55) of these companies outperformed the index. Globally, similar patterns are emerging. For example, between its inception in 2005 and December 2019, the Global 100 (G100), an index of the world's top sustainable corporations, has outperformed the MSCI ACWI (All Country World Index), returning 7.3% on an annualized basis, compared with 7.0% for the ACWI.

A Shifting Market Landscape

Structural shifts in the capital markets also helped move sustainable and impact investing from niche to mainstream. And two of these—both in the wake of the 2008–2009 financial crisis—did much to open up new opportunities. First, the rise of the passive investment industry changed the rules of the game by providing a stronger platform for activism. Second, the low-interest-rate environment dominating the postcrisis years pushed investors to seek yields in new markets and sectors.

In passive investing, the shift has been dramatic. These are index funds, whether mutual funds or exchange-traded funds (ETFs), which track financial market indexes such as the FTSE 100 or the S&P 500, an index of 500 large companies listed on stock exchanges in the United States. In August 2019, for the first time, US index-based equity mutual funds and ETFs surpassed active stock funds in volume, according to *Bloomberg*. "We have all seen the shift from active strategies to index-based strategies over the last decade or so, as many active managers have struggled to outperform their benchmarks and investors have focused more intently on fee productivity," said Cyrus Taraporevala, CEO of State Street Global Advisors, an asset manager with over $3 trillion in AUM.[23] "We think it has been a positive, democratizing development for millions of individual investors who can now gain low-cost access to markets around the world with ETFs and traditional indices in ways that were previously possible only for large, institutional investors."

The shift, he argues, has helped underpin the growing strength of sustainable and impact investing. "As one of the world's largest index managers, we own companies on behalf of our clients for as long as they remain in the index. That near-permanent capital status necessitates that we focus on long-term value so our clients can achieve their own long-term objectives," he said. "We have a very active stewardship practice that engages with global companies on a variety of material ESG issues, from effective, independent board leadership to climate change risk or aligning corporate culture with long-term strategy."

With the flow of money from active management to passive has come an unprecedented shift in the concentration of power to three big firms—BlackRock, Vanguard, and SSGA—that control more than 20% of the shares of typical S&P 500 companies, according to *Bloomberg*,[24] and manage assets worth more than China's entire GDP. This shift has also supported the growth of sustainable and impact investing in public equities, which has enabled a behavior change across entire industries that would not have been possible when deployment of investment money was through a fragmented sector of active managers.

The second postcrisis shift has been the low-interest-rate environment, prompting alternative investment firms, such as private equity firms, to deploy money in new ways to satisfy asset owners looking for yields—including viewing environmental sustainability and social impact as a means of driving growth and returns. In 2017, for example, TPG closed its $2 billion Rise Fund, giving it the largest pool of private equity capital dedicated to investing in companies that would return measurable social and environmental impact.

In 2010, Jessie Woolley-Wilson, an entrepreneur who describes herself as "a fallen banker" and who had spent time in New York tutoring middle school children as a way of giving back, joined an early-stage edtech company called DreamBox Learning, an online K–8 math program that uses its "Intelligent Adaptive Learning" technology to adjust teaching to students' individual learning needs and automatically offers them the right lesson at the right time. "I thought if I could bring my business acumen to a huge problem that was poised for disruption with technology, maybe I could help to democratize learning opportunities," she said.[25] "And I saw the power and the scalability of technology linked to content in an education environment."

This approach drew the attention of TPG's Rise Fund. In 2018, it made a $130 million investment in the company, which is among a range of enterprises in its portfolio whose businesses focus on everything from financial inclusion to access to healthcare and renewable energy. The Rise Fund uses the SDGs as a framework for its investments in companies that are delivering measurable positive social and environmental outcomes alongside competitive financial returns.

Since then, an investment strategy that was once the preserve of a small group of impact fund managers—such as LeapFrog Investments and Sonen Capital—has attracted giant private equity firms such as KKR, Bain Capital, Neuberger Berman, Natixis, Apollo, and Carlyle Group to create impact funds. Carlyle went even further in its statements. "If you make businesses better, they will perform better," Kewsong Lee, co-CEO at Carlyle, told *Bloomberg* in February 2020. "Impact is not a product or a way to grow assets. It should exist in everything we do."[26]

As the Rise Fund's approach illustrates, sustainable and impact investments are increasingly going beyond climate. However, climate change led the way, showing how other challenges could provide opportunities for investors to create social and environmental impact while generating a financial return. Indeed, the past few years have shown how quickly social issues can rise up the agenda. The #MeToo movement has, for example, forced companies to reexamine their gender equity policies and given added impetus to the growth of gender lens investing. As the field matures and as other issues capture public consciousness, an increasingly diverse range of human and environmental challenges will drive the sustainable and impact investing landscape forward.

The Risks of Rapid Acceleration

The momentum for this type of investing is excellent news. But amid the rush to develop new and transformative financial instruments, a key concern is ensuring the credibility and continued success of these products. And in the absence of widely accepted uniform standards for what constitutes a sustainable or impact investment, many so-called ESG-labeled funds may actually not be much different from any other market basket of funds. Even worse is what's known as "impact washing" or "greenwashing": funds claiming to be offering sustainable or impact investments but with no demonstrable or measurable positive social or environmental impact.

Another question is whether the sustainable and impact investing sector can continue to create credible and innovative vehicles that can attract capital at scale, while delivering impact that is real. This calls for ideas rooted in financial acumen, a rigorous and widely accepted understanding of how to define and measure impact, and effective practices for managing investment portfolios for impact. A similar challenge is whether the traditional problem solvers and new entrants to this arena, such as large companies, can continue to develop products and services that merit these types of investments.

The risks are not to be underestimated. Nor can the market alone provide all the solutions. Smart policymaking and financial regulation will be needed to ensure that the market for sustainable and impact investing avoids boom-and-bust scenarios or loss of investor trust. And we will need stringent levels of transparency and accountability in place to ensure that actions such as those that led to the rise and later dramatic collapse of private equity giant Abraaj do not occur. A healthy note of skepticism is a valuable asset—while we clearly want this new form of investing to succeed, we want to ensure it is built on solid ground.

With this caveat, we focus next on the stakeholders who are creating the new pools of funding to put to work for impact—individuals and organizations that form the heart of the financial system because they own or steward the money: asset owners. From individuals to giant institutional investors, asset owners shape the market through their investment preferences. And their preferences are increasingly shifting toward sustainable and impact investing. In the next chapter, we'll explain who they are and what they want.

Chapter 3

Asset Owners and What They Want

In 1969, just before Christmas in Norway, the country's fortunes changed forever. On December 23, the Norwegian government received a call from Phillips Petroleum (now ConocoPhillips) with news: The company had discovered a large oil field. This was something of a surprise. In 1958, the Norwegian Geological Survey had written to the Ministry of Foreign Affairs to say that there was no possibility of finding coal, oil, or sulfur on the continental shelf off the coast of Norway. Happily for the country, this assessment was wrong. Ekofisk turned out to be one of the largest offshore oil fields ever found. And it transformed the Nordic nation's fortunes.

Today, through the Government Pension Fund Global, the country's more than $1 trillion sovereign wealth fund, the proceeds of Norway's oil and gas industry help fund the country's generous welfare provision, which includes a universal healthcare system and free education for all. Though a rule limits annual withdrawal to no more than 3% of the fund's value, it is a critical source of money for the public budget. The fund supported the Norwegian economy after the 2008 financial crisis and again during the COVID-19 pandemic. Most of the fund's value today comes from investment gains, but of course, reliance on oil and gas revenues has also taken its toll. Concerns about the environment and, more recently, the effects of COVID-19 have led to a dramatic drop in demand, prompting a price collapse for these commodities. Even so, in May 2020, the fund enabled the country to plan a spending package of $41 billion to help it weather the economic downturn resulting from the crisis, according to *Bloomberg.*[27]

Norway's Government Pension Fund Global is one example of an asset owner. But they come in all shapes and sizes, from pension funds, insurance companies, and sovereign wealth funds to university and foundation endowments and high net worth individuals. Asset owners—also known as institutional investors and individual investors—have legal ownership of the capital and make asset allocation decisions based on their goals, investment objectives, and the market outlook.

Who Owns the Assets?

In this section we set out details for seven key groups: pension funds, insurance companies, sovereign wealth funds, development finance institutions, endowments, high net worth individuals, and the mass affluent. (Note: Double counting may occur, as we have sourced the data from different places.)

Pension Funds

- **Investor profile:** Asset owners responsible for paying pensions to many generations of retirees
- **Assets under management:** $46.7 trillion at the end of 2019, according to Thinking Ahead Institute's Global Pension Assets Study
- **Investment strategy and goals:** The longest of long-term horizons; steady returns that weather market turbulence; generally conservative, so an emphasis on liability-driven investment strategies that offer a secure, reliable income stream that covers all current and future payout obligations
- **Target for investments:** Mainly bonds and equities, although (seeking greater yields) many have expanded into riskier alternatives such as venture capital and private equity funds

- **Sustainable and impact investing:** A focus on portfolios that are not exposed to environmental and societal risks and that prioritize sustainable investments in high-growth, trusted economies
- **Investment management:** A mixture of internal investment teams and external managers

Insurance Companies

- **Investor profile:** Companies that pool premiums to offer protection against loss, with profitability largely driven by the success of investments made with clients' premiums
- **Assets under management:** $32.9 trillion in 2018, according to Statista research
- **Investment strategy and goals:** Generating income with premiums paid by policyholders before having to pay out claims and expenses; portfolios must match the predictability and time frame of their liabilities, taking into account relative duration and liquidity risk
- **Target for investments:** Across all asset classes but with heaviest reliance on fixed income
- **Sustainable and impact investing:** An increasingly important consideration, with greater focus on avoiding harm than on advancing impact
- **Investment management:** Largely through subsidiaries developed as part of the overall insurance group but with many outsourcing some or all asset management activities

Sovereign Wealth Funds

- **Investor profile:** The investment arms of nation-states
- **Assets under management:** The world's 10 largest funds hold just over $5.6 trillion, according to the Sovereign Wealth Fund Institute

- **Investment strategy and goals:** Amassing funds to protect and build national wealth by investing the money generated from oil or other commodities; with structural shifts in their economies and increasingly limited growth prospects for commodities such as oil and gas, the funds are of increasing fiscal importance to their owners
- **Target for investments:** Largely public equities (collective ownership of 6.3% of publicly listed equities globally), with a recent increase in allocation to alternatives (amounting to more than 15% of the global alternatives market, according to SSGA)
- **Sustainable and impact investing:** An emphasis on public equities with a focus on the *E* in ESG; funds in the West are most actively engaged, with 76% adopting an ESG policy in 2019, according to Invesco
- **Investment management:** A mixture of internal investment teams and external managers

Development Finance Institutions

- **Investor profile:** Government-backed institutions (either multilateral or bilateral) that invest in low- and middle-income countries
- **Assets under management:** About $87 billion in annual commitments in non-sovereign private-sector development financing in 2017, according to the Center for Strategic and International Studies
- **Investment strategy and goals:** To invest in sustainable projects that promote economic development and are increasingly focused on turning "billions to trillions" by working with the private sector
- **Target for investments:** Across all asset classes (although some may have certain restrictions); they are also able to offer guarantee instruments to facilitate investments that are otherwise too risky

- **Sustainable and impact investing:** Focus on advancing sustainable development through all their investments; the birth of new institutions such as the Asian Infrastructure Investment Bank and FinDev Canada has revitalized their global presence
- **Investment management:** Through internal investment teams

Endowments

- **Investor profile:** Funds typically used by universities to pay for their educational services and by foundations to make charitable donations in the form of grants
- **Assets under management:** Globally, philanthropic foundations hold $1.5 trillion, according to Harvard Kennedy School; the world's five largest university endowments hold $215 billion collectively, according to the Sovereign Wealth Fund Institute
- **Investment strategy and goals:** Perpetual investment horizon, with very few exceptions; US foundations, which must pay out at least 5% of the endowment in grants annually, seek a minimum return of 8% to make payouts and keep up with inflation
- **Target for investments:** Stable returns through diverse portfolios that have exposure to many asset classes, including substantial investments in alternative asset classes
- **Sustainable and impact investing:** A priority, and likely to become more appealing as increasing evidence of its positive financial performance emerges
- **Investment management:** Mostly external managers, with in-house teams used by some large institutions

High Net Worth Individuals

- **Investor profile:** Individuals with investable wealth exceeding a given amount (typically more than $1 million)

- **Assets under management:** More than $70 trillion in investable assets globally, according to Capgemini
- **Investment strategy and goals:** Generally to preserve intergenerational wealth and meet philanthropic goals
- **Target for investments:** The absence of the constraints facing institutional investors permits greater flexibility, enabling high net worth individuals to set longer time horizons, experiment with portfolios, make direct investments, and accept greater risk across asset classes
- **Sustainable and impact investing:** An increasing priority as the next generation assumes leadership
- **Investment management:** Through wealth management firms and family offices (personal investment firms for ultra-high net worth individuals)

The Mass Affluent

- **Investor profile:** Households with high incomes and growing assets but that are not "wealthy" in the traditional sense; part of an expanding cohort of business proprietors and affluent professionals
- **Assets under management:** $18 trillion in investable assets globally in 2019, according to Boston Consulting Group
- **Investment strategy and goals:** A wide range, from providing safety nets, creating savings for education, and generating income to preserving wealth
- **Target for investments:** More risk averse than high net worth individuals, with limited access to investments in the alternatives asset class
- **Sustainable and impact investing:** A strong interest in aligning investments with values
- **Investment management:** Many manage their own money through fintech platforms

The Shift Toward Impact

While they have diverse objectives, many asset owners share one thing: In recent years, they have been looking to meet more goals with their investments. Of course, they still want acceptable levels of risk and products that will deliver healthy financial returns. But on top of all this is another demand: sustainability and impact.

It is a shift in strategy that has ushered in a noteworthy change in practices across the entire investment industry, including asset managers and intermediaries. Figure 3.1 shows the many stakeholders that are part of the sustainable and impact investment landscape. Some asset owners have in-house asset management teams, while many outsource this by hiring asset managers to choose the right investments, act as fiduciaries, and invest in ways that achieve their goals. BlackRock has retained its position as the largest asset manager for over a decade now. Asset owners also heavily rely on intermediary firms, such as institutional investment consultants, investment advisors, and financial advisors—firms that

Figure 3.1. Sustainable and Impact Investment Landscape

Source: Bridgespan

hold considerable sway over where and how asset owners invest their money. One such example is Willis Towers Watson.

This evolution in asset owner strategy is perhaps not surprising. Since many asset owners are responsible for stewarding money that will benefit others, they see themselves as having a key role in society. As PensionDanmark's CEO, Möger Pedersen, said, "The young workers enrolled in our pension fund will go on retirement in 2070, and as average pensioners, they will receive income until the year 2100. So we have this incredibly long horizon and have to have a prudent take on how to invest long-term savings." This sentiment is shared by many of their peers. "The societal consensus in the Netherlands is that pension funds are there to contribute to societal good," said Claudia Kruse, managing director for global responsible investment and governance at APG Asset Management, which is responsible for investing funds that will provide pensions for more than 4.7 million Dutch citizens.[28] Today, asset owners want their managers to offer a widening range of options and increasingly see managers that fail to consider long-term sustainability value drivers—from climate action to human rights protection—as neglecting their fiduciary duty. And when the owners of the money speak, the managers of that money listen, something that is driving a wave of change through the entire financial system.

This was made abundantly clear in March 2020, when three of the world's most sizable pension funds—Japan's GPIF (Government Pension Investment Fund), the United States' CalSTRS (the California State Teachers' Retirement System, the country's second-largest fund), and the UK's USS (the Universities Superannuation Scheme, the country's largest fund)—issued a joint statement illustrating the increasingly prominent role of asset owners in promoting sustainable and impact investing. "Companies that seek to maximize corporate revenue without considering their impacts on other stakeholders—including the environment, workers and communities—put their long-term growth at risk and are not attractive investment targets for us. Similarly, asset managers that only focus on short-term, explicitly financial measures, and ignore the longer-term sustainability-related risks and opportunities are not attractive partners for us," the three wrote in their statement.[29]

The message was blunt. And in emphasizing the importance of long-term, sustainable growth, the statement marked a shift in approach across much of the financial industry.

Many asset owners have also been giving their managers ultimatums. In 2020, for example, Brunel Pension Partnership, a local government pension-scheme pool that manages £30 billion ($37 billion), gave its 130 asset managers a two-year deadline to reduce their exposure to climate change in line with the Paris Agreement. "Those that fail to do so will face the threat of votes against the re-appointment of Board members, or being removed from Brunel's portfolios when the partnership carries out a stock-take of its policy's effectiveness in 2022," said the company in its announcement.[30]

GPIF is also using its management fee structure to hold money managers accountable for ESG and impact outcomes, with evaluation based on stewardship activities that aim to enhance long-term value.[31] In 2018, the fund moved from a quantitative assessment framework to a qualitative one. Hiroshi Komori, senior director of stewardship and ESG in GPIF's Public Market Investment Department, told webinar attendees in June 2020 that this change reflects the behavior GPIF expects from its asset managers: "Be long term and think long term."[32] GPIF is not only applying ESG principles to the selection of a growing number of its own investments (something it says will continue despite the recent change in senior leadership), but it is also using its financial clout to raise sustainability standards across the entire market. It invests about 90% of its equity portfolio passively and is pushing index providers to hold companies accountable for their ESG performance.

Asset owners are also adding more stringent impact considerations to their due diligence criteria when selecting managers, including evaluating the way managers measure impact and their relevant technical resources and expertise. For example, GPIF no longer awards new mandates to money managers that lack ESG credentials.[33] Indeed, Bfinance, an investment advisor to institutional investors, found in its

2018 Asset Owner Survey that 10% of those responding had already terminated or changed managers owing to ESG considerations.[34] And in its response to the 2019 IPE survey of consultants who conduct manager selection, Bfinance highlighted ESG as "the most important driving trend in manager selection during the last five years." Similarly, David Hoile, head of asset research at Willis Towers Watson, said "some of the bigger and better asset owners talk in terms of strategic partnerships, which are quite interesting to look at in the way they turn a transactional asset manager relationship into something that's deeper and a bit more meaningful."[35]

While Hoile and his team see the commitment and capacity for building sustainable investments gaining increasing weight in the manager selection process, they also recognize the need for a nuanced approach to manager selection, since the way impact is generated differs between private and public markets. In the private markets, the focus would be on how asset managers source top-quality assets and whether they have the ability to enhance the impact and financial performance of the investment through monitoring and engagement with company management. Meanwhile, public equity asset managers are assessed on a different set of criteria, such as whether they have tools for executing proxy votes related to material ESG concerns.

In terms of issue areas, climate change remains the greatest focus for asset owners. However, many also want to have a positive influence in other areas, including gender equity, human rights, corruption levels, biodiversity, and resource efficiency. "Climate has dominated the SDG agenda and the impact investment industry and discussion," said PensionDanmark's CEO, Möger Pedersen. "But we should have a more holistic approach." This holistic approach is likely to gain momentum in the wake of COVID-19, said Hoile. "The principles of economic, corporate, and environmental resilience is a framing that will become much more important as we move between now and the next crisis," he said. "And what's interesting to us in terms of linking COVID and climate change or the natural environment is that they're all interlinked."

As asset owners become more strategic in their pursuit of sustainable and impact investments, they are asking new questions of their asset managers. These fall into four broad categories:

- *Philosophy,* such as the share of AUM made up of sustainable and impact investments, and whether ESG is incorporated into strategy and integrated across operations, with compensation structures incentivizing sustainability and long-term value creation
- *Process,* such as how ESG factors are incorporated into due diligence, whether active ownership practices are used to improve investment outcomes, and how organizational sustainability-related conflicts are addressed
- *People,* such as how responsibility for sustainability and ESG fits into organizational structure and whether sustainability and ESG expertise is limited to specialists or is the responsibility of everyone across the firm
- *Performance,* such as whether ESG and impact are part of portfolio risk/return assessments and how sustainability outcomes are measured

Driven by demand from asset owners, the vast asset management industry is working to create new opportunities for sustainable and impact investing across all asset classes. A 2019 survey conducted by the Morgan Stanley Institute for Sustainable Investing found that new AUM and investor expectations—alongside the potential for high growth—were among the top three drivers for firms and managers developing sustainable and impact investing strategies.[36] As a result, we are seeing a remarkable wave of innovation in sustainable products and strategies. In the next chapter, we will survey these and highlight some of the most promising.

Chapter 4

Strategies for a Sustainable Investment Agenda

As a firefighter, you often begin your workday with a long commute. On arrival at the station, a quick conversation with the off-going watch will tell you if there's anything to hand over. You might engage in some banter with colleagues, and perhaps a few jokes to help cope with the more stressful elements of the job. And this job is stressful. Whether it's battling a fire in a family's home or controlling a blaze on a derailed freight train whose shipment of toxic chemicals is putting a whole community at risk, you go to work every day knowing that your shift may bring you close to danger or tragedy. On top of all that, there is one more stressor: Chances are, you're spending more than half your income on rent.

It's not only firefighters who struggle with housing costs. America's housing affordability crisis means that teachers, nurses, social workers, police officers, and others—workers who provide some of our most essential services—are burdened with heavy costs. In the United States, almost one in two renter households spends more than 30% of their income on rent, while one in four spends more than half.[37] This limits people's ability to remain physically, mentally, and financially healthy, to pay for things such as education and training, and to achieve security in retirement.

Government programs and nonprofit sector initiatives have long tried to fix this challenging problem. However, three decades ago, one investor saw a solution he thought might make a difference. That was when K. Robert "Bobby" Turner joined forces with former basketball star Earvin "Magic" Johnson to create a series of funds—the Canyon Johnson Urban Funds—that would underwrite environmentally sustainable housing projects and other real estate investments to provide affordable options in urban communities while generating attractive financial returns for investors. "We were trying to focus on marketplaces that had been traditionally neglected, that were overlooked or misperceived, and that required unique skills to identify, quantify, and mitigate risks," Turner explained.[38] "And back then, by the way, we did not call it impact investing, we just called it smart investing." Turner came to this form of investing after working as one of three partners in one of the world's largest hedge funds. "I was definitely lacking the alignment between my values as a human being and my accomplishments," he recalled. "I struggled as a capitalist to find meaning. But as a philanthropist, I struggled to see impact as well."

In 2014, Turner, motivated by the success of his urban investments in both financial and human terms, launched his own firm dedicated solely to impact investing. Turner Impact Capital invests in community-serving real estate that improves access to high-quality housing, education, and healthcare in underserved urban areas throughout the United States. By harnessing market forces, Turner Impact Capital's investment funds have preserved more than 10,000 units of workforce housing, provided more than 44,000 low-income patients with access to affordable healthcare, and developed well over 100 campuses for top-tier charter schools in cities across the United States. Through an integrated approach, it creates companies, invests in them, and manages their activities. And with a track record of strong and consistent market rate returns, the firm has convincingly dispelled the myth that social impact and financial success cannot be achieved simultaneously. "We have 20 years of analytical proof to refute the notion that an investment can't do good and do well at the same time," Turner said.

Turner Impact Capital's investment model is now among a growing range of financial instruments—from money market funds and impact-rated bonds to private equity and securitization—that money managers use to deliver impact along with strong risk-adjusted returns. As a sector, they control very large sums of money. In 2019, discretionary AUM of the top 500 asset managers globally amounted to $91.5 trillion, according to Willis Towers Watson's Thinking Ahead Institute. In terms of asset classes, equity and fixed-income assets continue to dominate, with a 78% share of AUM. According to the institute, the total market divides into 43.6% equity, 34.4% fixed income, 6% alternatives, 7.7% cash, and 8.3% in other forms.[39] There are many characteristics that distinguish the asset classes from each other—not least the risk-return expectations of each. Asset classes with higher return potential carry higher risk, and vice versa. Figure 4.1 is a conceptual illustration of the trade-off between the long-term risk and returns of the various asset classes.

What's exciting is how money managers are using social impact and environmental sustainability as criteria for creating or adopting new financial products and innovative types of investment portfolios. However, innovation does not mean constantly reinventing the wheel. Traditional vehicles and tools can be adapted to accommodate sustainable and impact investment. But as this

Figure 4.1. Illustrative Trade-off Between Long-Term Risk and Returns of Common Asset Classes

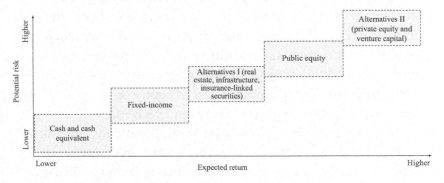

Source: From desk research—multiple articles, websites, and interviews.

chapter demonstrates, whether brand-new instruments or financial mechanisms repurposed for impact, the choice of strategies for investors seeking impact as well as financial returns is expanding rapidly.

Alternatives

In the early days of sustainable and impact investing, the players were small, new, highly innovative private market funds, often financed by development finance institutions, family offices, and private wealth clients. They tended to invest in early-stage or rapidly expanding companies and provided opportunities for investor involvement in shaping their growth trajectory. As the field has matured, however, larger venture capital and private equity investors have been attracted to the opportunities, with impact-labeled private equity funds deploying large pools of capital to a broad array of companies of significant scale.

Meanwhile, new types of insurance-linked securities have emerged on the alternatives landscape, allowing investors to take on natural catastrophe risks such as storms and wildfires in exchange for fixed yields with the principal returned after a period of three to five years, unless a catastrophe occurs. Opportunities for impact also exist in real estate investment trusts, or REITs (publicly traded companies with tax breaks that own income-producing real estate and pay dividends to shareholders), and renewable energy investment trusts (publicly listed companies that invest in renewable energy infrastructure such as wind farms to generate returns for investors). (While we recognize there is a debate about whether investment trusts should be classified as equity or alternatives, we are classifying them as alternatives in our overview.)

In fact, across the alternatives sector, innovation is flourishing, enabling a new generation of start-ups to scale up businesses delivering products and services that—from nutrition and healthcare to renewable energy—are having a positive impact on people's lives.

Venture Capital

While their funding is hard to secure, venture capital (VC) firms can kick-start enterprise growth. They invest in early-stage companies, often alongside other VC investors, and exercise control through representation on the board. Capital is raised in rounds, beginning with Series A and going through successively larger rounds until an acquisition or initial public offering. While few traditional VC firms are raising impact-specific funds, a growing number are investing in companies with groundbreaking ways of applying market models to social and environmental challenges.

San Francisco–based DBL Partners was a pioneer. Now with more than $1 billion in AUM, it invests in companies in sectors such as clean technology, mobility, sustainable products and services, healthcare, and information technology. It has, for example, invested in Apeel Sciences, a company founded to reduce food waste. Its protective coating of edible plant material slows the water loss and oxidation that cause spoilage, giving fresh produce a longer life.

Impact-focused VC funding can be found in both mature markets and the developing world. In March 2020, for example, Quona launched its $203 million Accion Quona Inclusion Fund, aimed at companies in emerging markets, while in October 2020, PayPal announced that it would invest $50 million in eight US Black- and Latinx-led VC firms, such as Harlem Capital and Vamos Ventures, as part of its efforts to support underrepresented minority communities.

Funds have different objectives, issue focuses, and investment styles. For some, it means identifying a gap in the market. According to a 2020 PWC report, climate is a sector with investment growth rates five times that of the other VC sectors.[40] As an example, launched in 2015, Breakthrough Energy Ventures (BEV) is an investor-led fund dedicated to investments for a "net-zero" world. With investors such as Bill Gates, Reid Hoffmann, Jeff Bezos, and Jack Ma, BEV invests in breakthrough climate solutions such as new battery storage technologies, water harvesting solutions, and technologies to capture and reuse carbon. It differs from other conventional VC funds by having a longer time horizon and partnerships with academic institutions.

VC firms tend to invest in high-growth segments that fit their focus and in companies that can deliver high returns (typically in the high double digits). While some have questioned whether venture capital can continue to generate these kinds of returns, Cambridge Associates found that the US VC industry delivered an average return of about 23% over the past 20 years. With higher-risk but potentially outsize returns over each investment's lifetime, funds typically attract institutions such as pension funds, insurance companies, sovereign wealth funds, and endowments, which allocate a moderate percentage of their total funds to these investments. While structured in different ways, VC funds aim to give investors downside protection (preventing a decrease in the value of the investment) while enabling the fund to make an additional investment at preferential terms if the company performs well.

Relative to demand from double-bottom-line entrepreneurs, VC capital remains scarce. In fact, a 2016 Stanford University Graduate School of Business research paper found that, on average, of every 100 potential opportunities they consider, VC firms only invest in one.[41]

Private Equity

While some private equity (PE) firms have been known as corporate raiders with a slash-and-burn approach, private equity's model of value creation—based on improving the companies in the firm's portfolio—is well suited to helping scale up impact-focused companies. They can therefore be an attractive funding source for double-bottom-line growth-stage companies and natural assets such as timberland and working forests, particularly now when traditional PE firms such as KKR, Bain Capital, Neuberger Berman, Natixis, Apollo, and TPG started creating dedicated social and sustainability funds focused on sectors such as agriculture, energy, education, health, and housing. PE firms generally take a stake in companies, exercise control through representation on the company's board (sometimes taking a direct role in management), and drive growth and rapid performance improvement—typically in two to six years—before selling the company.

While less risky than venture capital, private equity is also a high-risk investment proposition. Investors in PE funds are typically pension and sovereign wealth funds, endowments, and high net worth individuals. Given the higher risk to investors and high management charges, return expectations from this asset class are also higher. When assessing investment opportunities, according to Cambridge Associates, the US private equity index has delivered returns of about 11% over the past 10 years.

An example of how PE investment can help scale up the social impact of its portfolio companies is LeapFrog's 15% ownership investment in India's Mahindra Insurance Brokers in 2012. With the firm's investment, the broker was able to become India's third largest, enabling it to provide 8 million people—many of them rural workers—with property insurance, life insurance, and a health insurance product costing as little as 70 cents a month that covers an entire family's hospitalization costs. "No one has the reach of Mahindra into rural areas," said Andrew Kuper, LeapFrog's founder and CEO.[42] He explained that the firm pioneered the health insurance product in Ghana, "and when we applied it in India, they had a million people getting health insurance within three years." In 2017, LeapFrog sold its investment stake to XL Insurance Group, now part of AXA.

It was in 2017, with the closing of the $2 billion Rise Fund—founded by TPG, the PE firm, in partnership with Bono and philanthropist Jeff Skoll—that private equity for impact hit the headlines. As the Rise Fund has found, the number of innovative young companies to choose from when investing for impact is wide, compared with just a few years ago. The fund's investments include Acorns—a microfinance app that aims to financially empower the

182 million Americans making less than $100,000 a year, and the 69% lacking $1,000 in emergency savings—and ViewPoint Therapeutics, a biotechnology company developing treatments for diseases such as cataracts, which lead to visual impairment and blindness and affect more than 10 million people living in developing countries.

The fund helps its portfolio companies grow by offering capacity-building skills and access to its global network. It helps young businesses shape their narratives, giving them a better chance of attracting other investors. This was the case for Cellulant, a pan-African financial technology company that in 2018 secured a $47.5 million funding round led by Rise. Ken Njoroge, co-CEO and cofounder, explains that the investors helped the company focus on its business model: Was it a payments business or a software provider? Was it going to sell to banks or to merchants? "Frankly speaking, the story wasn't as neat as it is today," said Njoroge.[43] The Rise approach was a good fit for another reason: its ability to help the company achieve both commercial growth and impact. "You have a little bit of the patience of an impact investor with the pressure of a PE," said Njoroge. "The Rise Fund sitting inside TPG provided for us the attractive dynamic of a bridge in between that meant we could actually build a good business—but then that business would be fundamentally transformative."

Insurance-Linked Securities

Insurance-linked securities (ILS) are financial instruments whose performance is determined by loss events—typically low-frequency but high-severity natural catastrophes such as hurricanes and earthquakes. The most widely known ILS products, catastrophe bonds, were launched in the 1990s in response to the increased capital requirements imposed on the insurance industry after two large US natural disasters. Asset managers offering ILS products include specialized managers such as Fermat Capital Management, LGT Capital Partners, and Twelve Capital, as well as multiasset managers such as AXA Investment Managers and Amundi.

For problem solvers such as governments, ILS can be a way of transferring risk to private markets. If a catastrophe such as a storm, flood, or wildfire occurs within the time period set for a catastrophe bond, it can provide cash with which to fund recovery efforts, relieving the taxpayer burden. Since the securities are not linked to capital markets upheavals, they appeal to investors who want to hedge against sudden market shifts. For investors, the risk of losing the capital is offset by the promise that, in the absence of catastrophic events, they will reap attractive yields.

The US government embraced this approach in 2018, when the US Federal Emergency Management Agency (FEMA) used an ILS—a three-year catastrophe bond arranged with reinsurer Hannover Re—to offload the risk in its National Flood Insurance Program to the capital markets to the tune of $500 million, with an additional $300 million in 2019 and $400 million in 2020, according to the Artemis media service. For the latter issuance, the agreement was structured to cover 3.3% of losses for a given flood event of $6 to $9 billion and 30% for an event of $9 to $10 billion. The catastrophe bond supplemented traditional reinsurance coverage.

Social REITs

REITs are publicly traded companies that own income-producing real estate assets and pay dividends to shareholders, allowing investors to take equity stakes in real estate without having to acquire or manage the properties themselves. With returns based on underlying real estate assets, the reliable dividend income and long-term capital appreciation of REITs have long made them attractive to investors. While the largest REITs continue to hold traditional real estate investments, for those with impact in their sights, they also offer a mechanism through which to provide affordable and workforce housing.

In the UK, through Civitas Social Housing, one REIT is financing housing provision in England and Wales for people needing lifelong care and whose rent is paid from government housing benefits. Using capital raised from investors, Civitas Investment Management, Civitas Social Housing's investment advisor, buys homes tailored to residents' care needs, whether newly built, repurposed, or adapted from other residential homes. Rental income funds investor returns. For new residents, the effect of moving into social housing is transformational, said Andrew Dawber, group director at Civitas.[44] "Most of these people have been institutionalized for their entire lives," he said. "This is their first time living in noninstitutional housing." The model has allowed Civitas to produce an estimated £114 million ($142 million) in social value by increasing the supply and quality of social housing and improving the lives of vulnerable people.

Renewable Investment Trusts

With underlying assets such as solar or wind farms, renewable investment trusts are financing vehicles in which investors can buy and sell shares or reap dividends. In the case of some renewable investment trusts, assets include solar or wind farms with long-term fixed-price contracts with a local municipality, so returns are predictable.

One example is the Aquila European Renewables Income Fund. In June 2019, the fund raised more than €154 million ($173 million) when Aquila Group, a Hamburg-based independent asset manager, launched it on the London Stock Exchange. Most recently, in October 2020 it raised a further €127.5 million through a shares placement, according to S&P Global.[45] The fund invests in renewable energy infrastructure, such as hydro, wind, and solar generation technologies, across continental Europe and Ireland. Another is The Renewables Infrastructure Group, which is listed on the FTSE 250 and, with the largest generating capacity of the London-listed renewables investment companies, has a diversified portfolio of investments in more than 70 wind and solar farms across the UK and Europe.[46]

Cash and Cash Equivalents

In the early days of sustainable and impact investing, few might have included cash and cash equivalents as options for impact. But even cash in a bank account can be a tool for impact. And while few account holders currently do this, growing awareness of the effect that bank lending has on society and the environment may prompt consumers to demand that their deposits meet ethical or sustainability criteria. A few institutions are leading the way. For example, in the United States, Amalgamated Bank uses its deposits to support "sustainable organizations, progressive causes, and social justice."[47] And Europe's Triodos lends its customers' money only to organizations that are making a positive impact on communities and the environment.

Meanwhile, money-market funds, high-yielding funds that invest largely in short-term credit, can also be used for impact. At BlackRock, for instance, LEAF (the Liquid Environmentally Aware Money Market Fund) incorporates ESG factors into investment decisions. Considerations include the exposure of an issuer or its sector to environmentally damaging activities, the disclosures it makes on climate change and environmental issues, and its targets or plans to manage environmental risks. In addition, at least 5% of the net revenue from BlackRock's management fee from the fund is used to purchase and retire carbon credits. In July 2019, SSGA launched a similar product, the State Street ESG Liquid Reserves Fund, which offers investors a portfolio made up entirely of investments that met ESG criteria at the time of purchase.

The advantage of money-market funds and other cash-equivalent investments is that they can quickly and easily be converted into cash, making them the most liquid of asset classes. This means they are attractive to foundations, which need to pay out a required 5% in annual grants, as well as to insurers and pension companies with more significant payouts. Overall, their appeal among mainstream investors is on the rise. According to Fitch Ratings, AUM in ESG-focused money-market funds globally grew by about 30% across 35 funds in 2019 to a total of €70 billion ($79 billion).[48]

Fixed Income

At Saline County Career & Technical Campus, in a rural part of Arkansas, students can acquire a wide variety of vocational skills, from plumbing and carpentry to electrical skills and the ability to install, repair, and manage heating, ventilation, and air conditioning equipment. The college accommodates students who feed in from six school districts in the state. Funding for this project was made available through a bond issued in 2019 by Saline County for $43.53 million, a security that gives investors regular interest payments along with the return of the original amount invested when the bond reaches its maturity date.

"What they're teaching there are vocations that are extremely highly skilled, which we lack in this county, and that simultaneously provide extremely strong middle- and upper-middle-class-type occupations for people," said Stephen Liberatore, lead portfolio manager and head of ESG for the impact fixed-income strategy team at Nuveen, an asset manager with $1 trillion in AUM.[49] "So that's a project that is doubly beneficial in that it helps the county by providing skilled labor. It also helps individuals become more upwardly mobile."

Liberatore argues that for Nuveen, bonds such as this provide great opportunities for investors seeking impact. "They're measurable—we know how many people come out of the school, and we know the career paths that they take—but then they also look attractive from a total return perspective," he said. "That's kind of the combination we're looking for—the double bottom line of financial return, but also one that has direct and measurable impact."

The easiest way to think of a fixed-income investment such as a bond is as a loan that provides a steady stream of regular interest payments, along with a promise to return capital to investors at maturity. The coupon rate is determined by a number of factors, including the investment horizon (the longer the maturity, the higher the coupon rate) and creditworthiness (the higher the credit risk, the higher the coupon rate).

One of the largest asset classes under management, fixed income is popular with many institutional investors since it helps preserve capital and provides a predictable, steady income stream. As it tends to perform in the opposite direction of public equity markets, it also boosts portfolio diversification. Because of the stability of returns, investment-grade fixed income is considered a lower-risk investment and therefore has lower return expectations than VC or PE investments. For example, the Bloomberg Barclays Global Bond index has delivered a return of approximately 5% over the past 20 years.

Impact-Focused Bonds

For problem solvers such as governments and cities, fixed income is a useful tool since it offers access to funding for everything from affordable housing to clean technology upgrades and comes with one of the lowest return expectations. In 2017, for example, the Massachusetts Bay Transit Authority announced that it would issue about $574 million in tax-exempt sustainability bonds designed to pay for essential services and affordable infrastructure, health and safety improvements, and other projects with measurable socioeconomic benefits. The idea was to test whether issuing impact-focused bonds (as opposed to traditional municipal bonds) could lower the agency's borrowing costs, a hypothesis that was confirmed and translated into lifetime interest savings of about $2.60 per $1,000 issued.

Meanwhile, the high-grade debt issued by the World Bank and other development banks dedicated to social and environmental impact work in similar ways for governments in emerging markets. For example, the World Bank Group's International Bank for Reconstruction and Development (IBRD) issues bonds so it can lend to middle-income and low-income countries. Since the bonds come with the World Bank's stamp of credibility, they raise large sums of capital for development. In February 2020, for example, the bank used a global bond to raise £1.75 billion ($2.18 billion) from more than 100 international investors, the largest ever sterling-denominated bond issued by a supranational. The bank will use the funds to support its sustainable development activities, from improving global healthcare, nutrition, childhood development, and education to empowering society's most vulnerable groups, including women and the poor in rural areas. UBS and BlackRock are now also offering investors a single market basket of development bank bonds in the form of ETFs.

Green bonds are perhaps the most celebrated impact-focused bonds. They continue to raise large sums of money for government, development bank, and corporate climate-related projects. By 2019, almost $258 billion in green bonds had been issued, according to the Climate Bond Initiative.

Other types of institutions are seeing the potential for impact in the bond market. Seeing this as a way to increase the scale of its grant making in response to COVID-19, the Ford Foundation in June 2020 became the world's first nonprofit foundation to offer a labeled social bond in the US taxable corporate bond market. Net proceeds will allow Ford to make grants of more than 10% of the value of its endowment in 2020 and 2021—double the charitable payout required by US law.

ESG and Impact-Rated Bond Funds

Diversified fixed-income funds can also be created through the application of ESG screens to underlying fixed-income securities such as municipal bonds, corporate green bonds, or housing agency bonds. Investment management firm Brown Advisory does this through its Sustainable Bond Fund. It invests in corporate bonds, municipal bonds, and mortgage-backed and asset-backed fixed-income securities, which are issued as green bonds or meet ESG criteria, as well as in securities issued by the US government and foreign government entities.

A similar diversified product, Wellington Management's Global Impact Bond, invests primarily in investment-grade global fixed-income securities issued by entities such as corporations, governments, municipalities, and securitized issuers working to address social and environmental challenges. Across its multiasset impact platform, Wellington focuses on 11 themes related to major world problems—including agriculture, clean energy, and resource efficiency—and looks for investments that are trying to solve them. "Also we think that at least 50% of a company's revenue should be derived from goods and services that are solving one of the problems," said Campe Goodman, a senior managing director and fixed-income portfolio manager at Wellington Management.[50] "So there are some companies out there that are wonderful in terms of the business practices but, at least today, we would not include in our opportunities."

CDFI Bonds

For one group of institutions, the advent of new sustainable and impact investing financing mechanisms could prove particularly productive. For decades, community development finance institutions (CDFIs) have been working on the ground with marginalized communities, providing loans to low-income housing developers or small and medium-size businesses. However, CDFIs have had limited capacity to issue debt in the capital markets. This seems to be changing.

One signal of the potential was the July 2019 bond issuance of the Low Income Investment Fund. The $100 million sustainability bond (the offering included $25 million in 7-year bonds and $75 million in 10-year bonds) will be used to lend to nonprofits and mission-driven developers engaged in community development projects across the United States. Institutional investors showed keen interest in the bond, which S&P gave an A-positive outlook rating and was 10 times oversubscribed—demonstrating yet again the pent-up demand for high-quality fixed-income products that offer an opportunity to create tangible social and environmental impact.

Solar Asset-Backed Securitization

Securitization—which bundles different types of debt contracts, such as mortgages and credit card obligations—has not always been covered in glory, as was seen in the 2008 financial crisis, when banks repackaged and sold large amounts of bad mortgage debt. However, when used transparently and with a focus on social and environmental goals, this financial mechanism can unleash new capital for impact.

Take solar asset-backed securitization. This bundles together solar electricity payments such as power purchase agreement leases and loans that allow homeowners to install solar equipment. The first deal was made in 2013, when SolarCity, a solar energy services provider, issued a set of notes intended to raise $54.4 million to finance the company's expansion. Since then, the market has grown rapidly. The market has also expanded from pooling of purchasing power agreement leases to the packaging of solar loans. In one recent high-profile deal, Sunrun, a residential solar panel company, completed a second securitization of leases and power purchase agreements, which included $322 million in A-rated Class A notes.

Solar power is not the only way loan securitization can unlock new funds for impact. Similar models can be developed to increase investments in energy efficiency. In 2014, the Connecticut Green Bank paved the way for such deals when, after soliciting bids for aggregated projects, it selected Clean Fund, a capital provider, to purchase 80% of the $30 million portfolio in a groundbreaking deal for US commercial energy efficiency.

Using these kinds of mechanisms, problem solvers such as renewable energy companies and public sector agencies—organizations with underlying assets that lend themselves to securitization—can expand their operations and drive down the cost of capital by raising larger sums than they would otherwise be able to.

Public Equities

While a decade ago they may have seemed unlikely to yield impact, many public equities are now strong candidates for "positive inclusion" as the number of enterprises focused on sustainability increases. Investors can pick individual companies or invest in a fund whose portfolio managers make the investment decisions. These passive ESG investment products have proliferated, and many focus on areas such as gender equity and climate change.

Public Companies

As companies embrace sustainable business models, products, and services, it is increasingly possible to find attractive public equity investments that deliver impact as well as financial return. Examples include Ørsted—formerly known as Danish Oil and Natural Gas—which a decade ago started moving out of fossil fuels and began investing in the development and maintenance of offshore wind farms. Today it represents one quarter of the global market for offshore wind and has a market capitalization that surpasses that of traditional energy giants like British Petroleum and Equinor. To many it represents the future of the industry. As the head of equity research at Sydbank shared with Reuters, "All investors look at Ørsted and say: Here we buy into the future and when they look at the oil companies, including Equinor, they buy into the past."[51] Another Danish company, Vestas Wind Systems, which has profited from rising demand for renewable energy projects, ended 2019 with a record intake of orders, according to the *Financial Times*.[52]

New sectors are also providing public equity options. For example, in Denmark, biotechnology company Novozymes uses the SDGs to guide product development and corporate strategy. The company develops biological solutions to wastewater treatment and sludge reduction for municipal and industrial applications, helping improve access to clean water and sanitation. And its animal health and nutrition products help poultry and swine farmers increase their productivity more sustainably, helping eradicate hunger.

ESG Equity Funds

In advancing sustainable development, ETFs offer several promising features. As low-cost passive investing options, they enable investors to focus on a particular issue area or broader sustainability. And the choice of products targeting ESG factors has been widening over the past decade. The appeal of ESG ETFs—with their accessibility to individual and institutional investors—is something the biggest asset managers in the market have recognized. BlackRock has the world's largest ESG ETF. With assets of more than $10 billion, ESGU has been rated AA by MSCI through its ESG fund rating system, which measures the resilience of portfolios to long-term risks and opportunities arising from ESG factors.

Investment in equity ESG ETFs has grown sharply. Since the launch of the first ESG ETF in 2002, assets in ESG ETFs have reached almost $100 billion according to *Bloomberg*, evolving from the negative screening of "sin stocks" to overweighting companies prioritizing issues such as low carbon or gender diversity. As ESG integration gains momentum, active stewardship remains an important tool for encouraging companies to incorporate sustainability into their operations. Part of that strategy is to put laggards on notice, an approach SSGA is taking. In a letter issued to corporate board members in January 2020, CEO Cyrus Taraporevala said SSGA was prepared to take voting action against companies in the major stock-market indexes that have been "consistently underperforming" their peers in the R-Factor, SSGA's ESG scoring system.

SSGA has also employed more direct activism. For example, its 2017 Fearless Girl campaign, which called on boards to have at least one female director, was linked to research showing that companies with diverse boards perform better. As part of the campaign, SSGA commissioned the *Fearless Girl* statue that now stands in front of the New York Stock Exchange. The statue, which quickly gained attention since it was originally placed in front of the famous bronze *Charging Bull*, became emblematic of far broader gender-equality aspirations. Since SSGA launched its campaign, nearly 700 companies that previously had no women on their boards have appointed at least one woman.

Another approach money managers use is "investing in change," as those behind the WOMN ETF put it. WOMN tracks the Morningstar Women's Empowerment Index, which focuses on global companies that have policies, products, or services that rank highly against 19 criteria in four areas: gender balance in leadership and the workforce; equal compensation and work-life balance; policies promoting gender equality; and commitment, transparency, and accountability. Impact Shares, the nonprofit fund manager that issued the ETF, donates all its profits from management of the ETF to the YWCA, while the YWCA does the work of engaging with companies on how to implement and maintain strong gender-equality practices. Because the fund gives investors exposure to large and mid-cap companies, it enables them to achieve broad equity market returns while driving social change.

Meanwhile, the range of issues ETFs can address is also growing. For example, the Impact Shares NAACP Minority Empowerment ETF addresses racial inequality with criteria guided by the National Association for the Advancement of Colored People (NAACP). As Marvin Owens, NAACP's senior director of economic programs, told CNBC in June 2020, the ETF is "the next evolution in our corporate advocacy work around closing the wealth gap for African Americans in this country." At a time when everyone wanted to find out how to contribute, he said, "capital has the power to make social change."[53]

An Expanding Range of Options

As the examples in this chapter demonstrate, the choice of strategies for investors seeking impact and financial returns is widening rapidly, with countless new financial instruments being developed or adapted by money managers to social and environmental challenges. And given the size of the financial sector, the potential scale of the shift is tremendous.

However, while developing new products or repurposing existing ones is an important step, a tougher challenge is managing and measuring their impact. And while efforts to improve impact measurement are welcome, the plethora of tools and frameworks for impact and ESG reporting is creating confusion. In the next chapter, we will try to make sense of the "alphabet soup" of standards and metrics that investors need to navigate when trying to ensure and demonstrate to others that they really are investing for impact.

Chapter 5

How Do You Measure Impact?

Maryanne Hancock, CEO of Y Analytics, a company incubated within TPG's Rise Fund, points to an important shift in the evolution of impact measurement: Sustainable and impact investing now goes beyond intention alone. Today, she said, "there's so much information out in the world that can help us go from intent to confidence that something is going to have impact."[54] The question, however, is how to turn that information into intelligence.

This, said Hancock, was something the Rise Fund was determined to figure out. "What became very clear right out of the gate as they were designing the fund was that even though they were going to invest in collinear companies [in which financial performance and impact growth are aligned], the impact thesis would always be somewhat suspect if they didn't have a way to bring the impact story—the measurement of impact—forward very clearly," she said. "They needed decision tools to inform their due diligence and impact management that were grounded in evidence."

The challenge was that while investors often had access to social and environmental data on the companies in which they invested—from the number of people served and miles of land protected, to the amount of waste recycled—it was hard to quantify the benefits that would accrue to those communities and natural resources as a result of the investments. The solution was to turn to medical, scientific, economic, and other research to understand the expected effects. To make this kind of calculation, the Rise Fund partnered with consulting group Bridgespan to develop the Impact Multiple of Money (IMM), an innovative process that was refined and expanded with the Rise Fund's own in-house team and spun off. "They started out by saying they wanted to treat impact as rigorously as they treated the financials," said Hancock. "And that's what led them to the creation of Y Analytics."

The IMM process includes an initial qualitative screen that filters out companies with low impact potential as well as deeper screens that ask, for example, whether the company has social or environmental outcome targets linked to the SDGs and whether existing research and data verify that these goals are achievable and measurable. It also uses research that provides an evidence base for claims of impact and economic research to put a dollar value on the projected social or environmental change. Estimating the return on every dollar invested begins with assessing the total value that the investment is projected to create and then right-sizing it to reflect the investor's proportional ownership stake.

When the Rise Fund set out to deploy capital from its first fund, it committed to making an investment in a company only if the IMM calculation suggested that it would yield a sufficient social return. While the IMM generates a directional estimate of the potential extent of a company's social or environmental impact rather than a precise calculation, "the really fundamental piece is that we turn to actual research and data," said Hancock. Y Analytics and the Rise Fund have now expanded their decision tools to include those that are more relevant during hold periods, such as Impact Yield and Improvement Yield, which focus on annual impact and impact growth.

Now managed and expanded with ongoing research by Y Analytics, this evidence-based impact approach aims to give impact underwriting the same level of professionalization as financial underwriting by producing an impact return on investment figure. For while many sustainable and impact investors have worked to develop metrics for measuring impact, fewer have used rigorous tools to quantify the impact potential of an investment during the due diligence process. Hancock argues that this approach is the next essential step in sustainable and impact investment, since it allows the investors to determine how an investment will, in fact, affect the most critical elements of impact.

This evidence-based decision tool is among a wide range of efforts to professionalize the process of impact measurement. Sustainable and impact investment has moved from being an informal market built on personal trust to a broader industry that is attracting large-scale capital, creating the imperative to develop impact measurement systems with the credibility and integrity to inspire confidence in mainstream investors.

The Field Expands

Until recently, nonprofits and public-private partnerships led most of the efforts to standardize impact measurement. An early development was the Global Impact Investing Rating System (GIIRS), now administered by B Lab, the nonprofit that also certifies B Corporations, which are audited for their impact on employees, customers, suppliers, the community, and the environment. GIIRS's scoring focuses on companies' social and environmental "returns."

To enable apples-to-apples impact comparisons, the Impact Reporting and Investment Standards (IRIS)—developed in 2009 and hosted by the GIIN—established common terms and standardized definitions for a range of impacts. Other initiatives include the Global Reporting Initiative (GRI), the Sustainability Accounting Standards Board (SASB), the Climate Bond Initiatives, and the Task Force on Climate-Related Financial Disclosures (TCFD), which is developing voluntary standardized disclosures that companies can provide to investors, lenders, insurers, and others.

Today, ratings agencies such as Moody's and S&P Global Ratings are joining asset managers and advocacy groups and, more recently, artificial intelligence companies in developing sustainability ratings and rankings. Many are using acquisitions to advance their measurement capabilities. For example, in 2018 Moody's acquired Vigeo Eiris, an ESG research firm; the following year it bought a majority

Figure 5.1. Landscape of Sustainability Information Providers

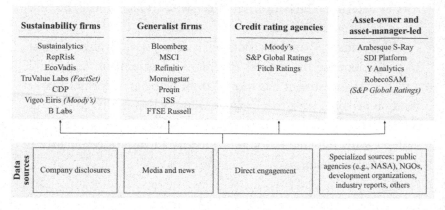

Sustainability firms	Generalist firms	Credit rating agencies	Asset-owner and asset-manager-led
Sustainalytics	Bloomberg	Moody's	Arabesque S-Ray
RepRisk	MSCI	S&P Global Ratings	SDI Platform
EcoVadis	Refinitiv	Fitch Ratings	Y Analytics
TruValue Labs *(FactSet)*	Morningstar		RobecoSAM
CDP	Preqin		*(S&P Global Ratings)*
Vigeo Eiris *(Moody's)*	ISS		
B Labs	FTSE Russell		

Data sources	Company disclosures	Media and news	Direct engagement	Specialized sources: public agencies (e.g., NASA), NGOs, development organizations, industry reports, others

Source: From desk research—multiple articles, websites, and interviews.

stake in Four Twenty Seven, a climate research firm that provides data and analysis on physical climate risks, including information enabling evaluation of local government preparedness to manage climate risks such as floods, fires, and storms, which means it can rate municipal bond issuances more accurately.

Also in the measurement business are sustainability-focused firms such as Sustainalytics and RepRisk, generalist data providers such as ISS and MSCI, and asset-manager-led solutions such as Arabesque S-Ray and Y Analytics. In fact, research from Opimas, a global distributor and service provider, predicted that by 2021 investors would be spending $1 billion on ESG tracking. Many are competing to come up with the leading tool—the one all investors will eventually use. Figure 5.1 shows the crowded landscape of companies competing for the lucrative market.

A Complex and Crowded Landscape

With the development of new measurement tools and approaches, however, a new problem emerged: variations in the data's quality and relevance. "The biggest challenge with integrating sustainability or ESG considerations into investment decision-making is the data disarray," said SSGA's Cyrus Taraporevala. "While almost 90% of S&P 500 companies now issue corporate social responsibility reports, the data are all over the place. At the same time, companies are frustrated by the multiple questionnaires they receive from ESG data providers, each asking slightly different versions of the same questions."

Diverging taxonomies, standards, metrics, and ratings can result in the same investment ending up with a different sustainability profile from different rating firms. Ratings agencies, for example, assess the E (environmental), the S (social), and the G (governance) in ESG using different methodologies. And they don't give the same weight to each of the three elements. Moreover, since methodologies diverge, it becomes hard to make comparisons.

This was illustrated in a 2018 article in the *Wall Street Journal* that compared the ESG ratings of companies such as Tesla and Exxon by different ratings agencies and found that Exxon received a higher overall rating from two of the three largest ESG ratings firms.[55] Of course, as some have pointed out,[56] few investors would compare a vast multinational energy company with an entrepreneurial carmaker. However, the article also highlighted the fact that few agree on what constitutes a high sustainability score. And each of the three ESG variables differed greatly between Tesla and Exxon and may matter differently to investors, depending on their impact goals.

MIT found the same in 2019, when it reported that the six leading ratings agencies disagreed on ESG ratings at three levels: selection of different sets of categories, measurement divergence related to different assessment of ESG categories, and the weight of divergence related to the relative importance of categories in the computation of the aggregate ESG score.[57]

All this has led to growing exasperation among both companies and investors. The Institute of International Finance (IIF) recently highlighted the challenges. In March 2020, it warned that in becoming a catalyst for the move to a sustainable economy, the financial system was facing a significant barrier: fragmentation in the regulation, supervision, standard-setting, and ratings systems used to make climate risk assessments. "The absence of an international standard or guidelines," the IIF authors wrote, "appears to be leading to a high level of experimentation at the national level that can lead to or exacerbate fragmentation."[58] The toll has become clear: In one IIF study, lack of standardization came out as the number one reason for not disclosing data on emissions, with about 44% of respondents citing it. And while the IIF report focused on climate change, its points apply across the sustainable and impact investing landscape.

Some progress has come on harmonization and coordination. In July 2020, SASB and the GRI announced a collaboration "to help stakeholders better understand how the standards may be used concurrently."[59] The European Union is working on standard taxonomy and disclosures for the European market, and in the United States the SEC may, after years of debate, finally address the issue. In addition, the Impact Management Project, which convenes more than 2,000 practitioners and coordinates industry-wide projects, is working to build international consensus on how to measure, compare, and report on the risks and positive impacts of ESG factors and to agree on norms for a wide range of technical topics. However, given the woeful track record of international collaboration on everything from global trade to COVID-19 containment, full global coordination is unlikely, at least in the short term.

Meanwhile, many methodologies are backward-looking in nature rather than assessing current performance or future risks and opportunities. And the critical issue of materiality is far from settled. Materiality factors—those that have an impact on financial performance, positively or negatively—differ across asset classes. For example, something considered a material factor when investing in the stock of a publicly traded European company is not necessarily material when investing in a short-term bond issued by an African country. Investors also remain torn between the need for standardization and a desire for customization, and disagree on whether we need industry-wide scoring systems or sector-specific benchmarks.

Unsurprisingly, given the complexity of the impact measurement landscape, investors are using the tools in different ways. In a 2020 Rate the Raters survey by SustainAbility, many large asset management firms said they frequently used ratings from multiple providers. The survey also found that, to differentiate themselves, most asset managers had their own tools and metrics, and third-party ratings were one of multiple data points for analysis.[60]

So how can asset owners, money managers, and problem solvers overcome the data disarray and navigate a standards and metrics maze that can seem overwhelming? While the landscape undergoes rapid change and promising solutions emerge, it is too soon to pick winners. We believe the best approach is to focus on three key areas: materiality, use of technology and online platforms, and an integrated impact management approach.

Materiality at the Core

As more money moves into sustainable and impact investing, a key question is this: What will create maximum value and protect from risk? Answering this question means figuring out which impact factors will be material to an investment. And while there's no shortage of data and analysis, the challenge is finding the right answers for each asset class. The problem was summed up in a BNP Paribas report in a quote from Ian Woods, head of ESG Research at AMP Capital. "Data is the easy bit. Analysis is the relatively easy bit. It's the 'so what' in each asset class that is the challenge," he said. "But answering the 'so what' question is different in a credit portfolio than it is in an equities portfolio. Those analysts think in very different ways."[61]

SASB has gone some way toward establishing the "so what" in different sectors. It has developed a set of sustainability accounting standards covering material issues for 77 industries.[62] Innovation has also come from SSGA, which in April 2019 launched its R-Factor system, a scoring tool developed in partnership with SASB, for assessing listed companies according to their ESG practices. The system uses the SASB Materiality Map, a framework that identifies material ESG issues ranging from greenhouse gas emissions to labor practices and business ethics and categorizes them according to industry. "The R-Factor—'R' for responsible—scoring system provides a transparent and comparable ESG assessment of companies based on information that matters to investors," said SSGA's Cyrus Taraporevala. It is important, he said, "to ensure that investors are approaching sustainability with the same rigor that applies to other forms of investment risk."

Some in the investment community have worked to determine the materiality of sustainability factors for other asset classes. For example, ESG is an important factor in the performance of emerging market sovereign debt. Emerging market countries that perform poorly on ESG factors tend to pay a higher market premium to issue debt, and vice versa.

To capture this, Caisse des Dépôts et Consignations (CDC), a French public-sector financial institution, has developed an in-house proprietary methodology assessment tool to evaluate the material risk of ESG in its sovereign debt emerging market portfolio. According to a UNPRI case study,[63] the CDC approach uses ESG indicators such as forestry, energy, agriculture, water, and air quality (for E); the Gini coefficient (a measure of income inequality) and education and health indicators (for S); and government effectiveness or levels of corruption, with a focus on gender equality (for G). This method diverged significantly from the CDC's traditional approach, based on macro fundamentals such as solvency, refinancing capacity, growth, and revenues, with decisions largely driven by major credit rating agency opinions.

The shift led to changes in the CDC's portfolio. For example, it removed a sovereign bond whose ESG materiality assessment raised questions about the issuer's financial performance. The bond's E risks included relatively poor performance on air quality, carbon emissions, and greenhouse gases in the agricultural sector. And its G performance, on gender equality, was poor, with little sign of efforts to improve this. Two major ratings agencies downgraded the issuer by one notch four to six months after the CDC decided to remove it from the portfolio.

As investors focus on materiality factors, they are using different methodologies and place emphasis on different things. However, across the investment industry there are signs of progress. While in 2017 a GIIN investor survey found 35% highlighted impact measurement and management practice as a challenge (just 11% saw progress in this area), in the 2019 GIIN survey, 80% saw "some" or "significant" progress. The good news is that if this trend continues, we are on the path to better integration of materiality into investment decisions.[64]

Technology and Intelligence-Based Platforms

Gone are the days when ESG data were limited to simple yes-or-no answers on whether companies had carbon emissions or human rights policies. Now, new technologies make it possible to collect up-to-date (even real-time), relevant, and consistent data that are both quantitative and qualitative. From machine learning to artificial intelligence and satellite imagery, these technologies will facilitate intelligence based platforms and generate better quality of data and insights, greater accuracy, and the possibility of applying artificial intelligence to historical data.

For ratings agencies, analysis of geospatial data (which have geographic and locational elements) is improving evaluation of climate risks. For example, S&P Global Ratings recently used information collected by NASA satellites to examine whether the location of public water utilities would affect their financial resilience. According to *Bloomberg*, S&P found a correlation between utilities located in ecosystems such as evergreen forests, which foster improved water quality, and better metrics on debt.[65]

Satellite imagery is a particularly powerful tool when combined with other data sources. One example is its use by the Land Degradation Neutrality (LDN) Fund, an impact investment fund focused on the rehabilitation of degraded land by financing the transition to more sustainable land use. Managed by Mirova, an ESG-focused investment firm and affiliate of Natixis Investment Managers, the fund invests in projects that deploy sustainable land management practices. Since projects without the required collateral struggle to secure funding from risk-averse local banks, the fund bridges two worlds—between early start-up and established business funding. As part of its impact measurement process, LDN Fund uses satellite imagery technologies, such as Trends.Earth, an online tool developed by Conservation International. The Trends.Earth platform uses satellite imagery and global data to monitor reductions or losses in the biological or economic productivity of land, informing decision-makers and investors on how and where to deploy resources.

In another initiative—led by Dutch pension fund management institutions APG and PGGM, which collectively manage more than €780 billion ($787 billion)—asset owners themselves have created an online platform to help assess the social and environmental impact of public equity investments. The SDI Asset Owner Platform combines sustainable development investment taxonomy with artificial intelligence to generate insights into how the commercial activities of public companies are contributing to meeting the SDGs. "We developed a detailed rule book—sector by sector—on how we can identify a contribution to the SDGs," explained APG's Claudia Kruse. "But we realized it was impossible to do the work manually. We were then in touch with the data science team of Deloitte, which developed a proof of concept we liked. After that their data science team spun out of Deloitte and became Entis, an AI tech platform with APG as a majority owner."

Technology can never replace human evaluation entirely, particularly when it comes to complex social issues. Eventually, however, as in so many industries, digital technologies will take over many of the mundane review processes, conduct analysis with speed, and allow humans to apply their analytical powers to more complex decisions.

Impact as an Integrated Management Practice

Of course, more data do not guarantee improved intelligence. Asset managers also need to understand and interpret the data and consider impact return and financial return in a more integrated way. This means moving from a purely metrics-based discipline to a practice with a broader concept: impact management.

Christina Leijonhufvud, managing partner of the advisory group Tideline, sees impact management as a newer narrative shaped around investor expectations. "It's a process for monitoring the progress of each investment against the expected impact and, most importantly, engaging with investees when they are not meeting their targets," she said.[66] "And then, finally, you need a system for measuring and reporting on impact, reviewing results, and making improvements to the impact management system based on lessons learned."

Recognition of the need for an integrated approach prompted the launch in 2019—initially with 60 signatories—of the Operating Principles for Impact Management (OPIM) by the International Finance Corporation (IFC). These nine principles focus on transparency, credibility, and disciplined impact management. The principles, developed in collaboration with investment industry representatives from across the globe, aim to enable impact considerations to be integrated into the entire investment process, from deal origination and structuring to exit. While prescribing no specific tools or approaches, the principles provide investors with a framework that enables them to learn from each other as they implement them. Asset managers can adopt them for specific sustainable or impact funds or for their entire assets.[67]

By 2020, the principles had more than 100 signatories, from large asset managers such as Amundi and BlackRock to development finance institutions such as the Dutch agency FMO and the UK's CDC Group. While theoretically the approach can be applied to all asset classes, its initial focus has been on private equity. Hans Peter Lankes, the IFC's vice president of economics and private-sector development, points out that there has been more experience in building impact management systems for private equity. "When it comes to public equities and fixed income, it is harder," he said.[68] "But that is where the big numbers are."

Some have worried that the principles amount to little more than window dressing. To address these concerns and ensure true accountability, signatories must sign up for independent verification, which, according to Lankes, has been by far the most discussed principle. In April 2020, Tideline published the first of the verification reports and shared best practices and areas for improvement based on 13 verifications. One area in need of improvement, it found, was that insufficient understanding of the social and environmental context surrounding their investments could lead investors to overstate the likely scale or depth of their capital's impact. "Impact investors should try to fill in the gaps in their understanding using market research to enable realistic impact target setting and mitigate both impact and financial risks," wrote Tideline.[69] While this verification practice can undoubtedly create more accountability, it can be quite expensive, something the OPIM steering committee is working to address.

The Path Ahead

Systems for measuring impact underpin the ability of the financial sector to act as a catalyst in the transition to a sustainable global economy. At a minimum, impact measurement is needed at two points: early in the investment decision-making process (origination and due diligence), and then to ensure investments are having the intended impact.

Despite the current confusion, we believe impact measurement will ultimately standardize and harmonize as investors demand mechanisms for making comparative investment decisions and for reporting on the impact of their investments. This is important. The higher the quality and the more credible impact measurement becomes, the more confidence investors will have in putting increasing amounts of money into sustainable and impact investments.

So far, we have presented the state of the sustainable and impact investing landscape and some of the industry actors and developments that have accelerated its growth. However, as funders, field builders, and practitioners, we know that understanding the promise of sustainable and impact investing is just the first step. In the next section, chapters 6 and 7 will explore some of the steps problem solvers and money managers need to take both to participate in and to expand this exciting new market. Then, chapter 8 highlights challenges that may arise when these two groups come together and shows how they can find the right partners and make the match a success. By offering practical advice and answers to key questions, we hope to help turn inspiration into action.

PART II

The Players

Chapter 6

The Problem Solvers

As a global conservation NGO, WWF (once known as the World Wildlife Fund) is well aware that some of the world's most valuable raw materials exist in regions home to some of the poorest communities and the most fragile of ecosystems—environments put at risk when mining operations move into these areas. NGOs are an example of what we call the problem solvers, which have long tried to influence companies in the extractives sector to reduce these negative impacts. But the question WWF asked was this: What if the risk of damage could be minimized, and potential social benefits specified, far earlier in a project's development by engaging more directly with companies and investors?

This was the impetus behind the creation of WWF-SIGHT, which is a spatial land-use mapping tool (the organization calls it "conservation intelligence") developed by WWF-UK and WWF-Norway. This tool—integrating commercial mining data sets—makes it possible to see where mining activities and concessions overlap with areas of natural and social importance in order to engage with stakeholders, including investors, to mitigate any potential damage these projects may cause. "We came at this realizing we had very little information on where future mining, and oil and gas would take place," explained Susanne Schmitt, nature and spatial finance lead at WWF-UK.[70] "You're always on the back foot. Once you find out, it's often too late, many millions of dollars have been sunk into a project, and all you can do is tinker around the edges."

Insights from WWF-SIGHT have been used in joint research projects with financial institutions such as Investec Asset Management and Aviva Investors, which in 2015 in collaboration with WWF produced the *Safeguarding Outstanding Natural Value* report. "We've engaged all the way along because there's a lot of interest in metrics and data," said Schmitt. "And there is a huge potential because, with some companies, you might do your due diligence analysis and have pointers from a financial point of view. But analysis combining environmental and asset-level data—geo-located concessions or operations with ownership information—highlights a company's risk (related to both its impacts and its dependencies) on nature and the environment, adding important additional information on sustainability."

Some problem solvers are working even more closely with money managers to develop new tools. For example, in 2010, when the private equity firm Carlyle Group wanted to develop a due diligence methodology to assess the environmental risks and opportunities of potential acquisitions, it turned to a nonprofit, the Environmental Defense Fund (EDF). The result was EcoValuScreen, a tool developed in partnership with global environmental consultancy the Payne Firm that builds on Carlyle's due diligence practices and EDF's Green Returns framework for improving environmental performance of investments. To spread the tool's impact, the EDF partnership included an agreement that Carlyle would publish information about the methodology on EDF's website.[71]

As the WWF and Carlyle initiatives demonstrate, the insights, knowledge, experience, and credibility of problem solvers provide immense value to money managers. Problem solvers can provide technical assistance and act as trusted advisors to companies and investors. They can also present their own investable propositions. However, to have the desired impact, problem solvers need a good understanding of the financial sector, the way it works, and the objectives it needs to fulfill.

How Can Problem-Solving Entrepreneurs Strengthen Their Investment Propositions?

For start-ups and growth companies looking to raise capital, the challenge is passing muster in investors' financial *and* impact due diligence processes. During the impact due diligence, all are trying to answer three basic questions: What degree of societal impact is this investment likely to deliver? How does it mitigate negative externalities? Is it sufficient to deem this an investment worth making?

Such rigor can be helpful to the development sector, says SeyCCAT's Angelique Pouponneau, with whom we talked in the introduction. "I like what the private sector brings to this space," she said. "There's a level of needing to be able to measure impact, because people want to know what's happening with their money. It's not just about [investors] giving the money and saying goodbye— it's what their money is being used for and the difference it's having in the development sector. That's really important because it's keeping us all aware and accountable."

Since sustainable and impact investors are devising metrics that allow them to ask whether the investment yields a benchmark amount of impact, entrepreneurial companies seeking capital must convince them that they can deliver sizable, measurable impact as well as profit—or at least are on a path to doing so. This means understanding investors' impact goals and knowing what to expect from the diligence process.

The process varies by manager. In chapter 5, we described the Y Analytics impact metrics used by the Rise Fund. Another approach is that of LeapFrog Investments, one of the largest dedicated impact managers with a portfolio of financial services and healthcare companies reaching more than 200 million people in emerging markets. To assess investment opportunities, LeapFrog applies a proprietary tool called FIIRM—Financial Performance (F), Impact and Innovation (II), and Risk Management (RM). The II and RM components are assessed against a company's nonfinancial and financial benchmarks for scale, quality, affordability, and governance, and the assessment is calibrated using market data on consumers. The framework correlates positive financial returns with companies that also generate social impact and is used not only for measurement but also for driving and improving integrated financial and impact performance.[72]

LeapFrog founder and CEO Kuper stresses that financial and nonfinancial data must be integrated. He cites insurance renewal ratios, which are highly quantifiable. "If people are not coming back and buying your product, you have a massive financial problem, because it's much more expensive to get a new customer than to keep one," he explained. "You have a massive social problem, because they obviously are not seeing much value in this apparently essential service or product that you have to offer. You have a significant risk because you're losing huge parts of your book. And clearly there's a need to innovate and change to make sure that renewal ratio fundamentally transforms." In this way, he adds, financial, impact, risk, and innovation considerations are aligned and can be tracked and driven using a standard industry metric.

Some firms set impact benchmarks in outcome categories by investment domain. This is the case for Equilibrium Capital, a sustainability-focused global asset management firm that is both a fund manager and an operator of sustainable assets such as farms. It evaluates the impact potential of companies in five categories: capital, energy, water, jobs, and carbon. It used this framework when it invested in Minnesota-based Revol Greens. The company's farming techniques rely on natural light, filtered rainwater, and snowmelt, as well as technologies such as a hybrid hydroponic system that uses soil and nutrient-rich water to grow produce year-round. Its operations also capture carbon dioxide and turn it into fertilizer.

Diligence processes can be lengthy. For example, SJF Ventures—a US VC firm focused on high-growth companies in sectors such as recycling, sustainable agriculture, mobility, smart infrastructure, education, and health—assesses companies for their degree of intervention, scale, degree of need, efficiency, and sector-level impact.

When it led Series B financing for NEXTracker, whose technology enables solar panels to generate more energy by tracking the sun's movement, it engaged in diligence with the company for a year before the investment.

However, while the process may be arduous, when problem-solving entrepreneurs meet investors' expectations, the prize is large-scale funding. Take education, a critical component of building socially and economically healthy and vibrant communities. In 2019, for example, US edtech firm 2U acquired VC-backed Trilogy Education Services, which provides digital skills training, for $750 million, according to TechCrunch. And DreamBox Learning, the online K–8 math program, had by 2020 raised $175.6 million in six rounds, according to CrunchBase.[73] Armed with such funding, entrepreneurs can turn ideas into transformational businesses.

What Can Public Companies Do to Attract Investors Seeking Impact?

For public companies, the imperative is to build a sufficiently robust performance record to attract investors looking for sustainable and impact investment options. To be included in the investment products being launched and scaled, companies must exceed the threshold in two areas: improving ESG performance generally, and shifting to new business models that embed issues such as equality or sustainability into every aspect of the enterprise.

Improving ESG Performance

When looking to improve, companies should identify the ESG factors material to their business—both now and in the future—those that drive risk reduction, productivity, and growth. If material and verifiable factors are present, best-in-class companies set ambitious sustainability goals and ensure they are meeting strict standards in areas such as gender equality, resource efficiency, and climate action. As investors and regulators toughen requirements—including on corporate ESG disclosure—ESG principles must be thoroughly integrated into business activities.

For example, to be included in the UBS Global Gender Equality UCITS ETF (GENDER SW), companies must be able to show their commitment to gender diversity—and it's no longer sufficient to focus on board-level female representation. To assess companies as targets for investment, GENDER SW uses as a benchmark the Solactive Equileap Global Gender Equality 100 Leaders Index, which tracks corporate leaders in gender equality internationally. Its methodology, made up of 19 criteria, assesses companies' leadership and workforce gender balance, equal compensation and work-life balance practices, policies promoting gender equality, and transparency and accountability commitments.

Integrating ESG principles across a company's operations means demonstrating how social and environmental practices can improve performance and make the enterprise more resilient—whether through resource efficiencies or increasing the productivity of employees and suppliers. For example, Fibria Suzano, a Brazilian eucalyptus pulp producer (a subsidiary of Suzano Papel e Celulose, one of the world's leading suppliers), developed an innovative model that provides income for smallholder farmers by integrating them into its supply chain for eucalyptus wood. Through its Forest Savings Program, it promotes biodiversity protection while it applies predictive analytics tools and big data to its wood production processes to foster regrowth, which uses postharvest natural tree sprouting to give rise to new forests.

Business Model Shifts

The real opportunity for companies—and something investors are increasingly seeking—is to reshape the core strategy, transforming the ability to deliver positive social and environmental impact while increasing prospects for superior long-term financial results. Creating social impact through innovative and profitable business models and/or new, higher-impact products and services helps companies get ahead of the competition, meet future social and environmental regulations, and attract a growing cohort of social and impact investors.

Koninklijke DSM, a Dutch life sciences and materials sciences corporation focused on nutrition, health, and materials (a corporation included in Corporate Knights' 2020 ranking of the world's 100 most sustainable corporations), has developed a reliable stream of profitable innovations by focusing on solutions that advance SDGs such as ending hunger, promoting health and well-being, and ensuring sustainable production and consumption.

Other companies have made more radical transformations, shifting away from any product with a negative impact and repurposing assets and operations to meet demand for sustainable products or services. Starting in the 1990s, for example, Belgium-based Umicore, a materials technology group, made significant investments to transform itself from a mining business into a recycling company that recovers metals from waste such as circuit boards, mobile phones, and other products, increasing the resource efficiency of materials that can be associated with labor abuses and environmental degradation.

As impact measurement improves and investors build increasingly sophisticated sustainable and impact investment portfolios, companies wanting to position themselves as attractive investments must demonstrate that they are going far beyond traditional, siloed ESG thinking and tying social and environmental impact directly to competitive advantage and economic performance.

How Can Nonprofits Create Double-Bottom-Line Investment Propositions?

Problem solvers such as NGOs, foundations, and development organizations did not traditionally work with financial markets. This is changing. It's now clear that they can engage with markets in two ways: Those with programs that solve social and environmental challenges can turn those into investable or insurable propositions.

And—through research and thought leadership, advocacy, and technical assistance—they can help shape sustainable and impact investing markets.

Of course, not every cause in need of capital is an investable or insurable proposition. A 2017 study linking the SDGs to investment opportunities provides insights into what may work and what may not. The study (by Dutch pension managers APG and PGGM) found that 2 of the 17 SDGs—peace and justice, and partnerships for the goals—had no prospects for private investment. Even within the 15 goals identified as having investment potential, the study found that not every subgoal lent itself to a proposition for investment capital.[74]

However, when the goals without a current investment prospect were divided into "emerging and investable," the study concluded that many could attract private capital in the future. The APG-PGGM research can help problem solvers assess whether their program or project has the potential to attract double-bottom-line investment capital. Then, problem solvers must ensure it meets investor expectations in four areas: financial viability, fitness for impact, standardization, and size and track record.

Financial Viability

To attract for-profit investors at scale, all investable programs and projects need to be capable of delivering a return, whether through anticipated cash flows or expected multiples at exit. And while alternative energy, affordable housing, and sustainable agriculture have typically been sectors most readily able to meet this criterion, they are not the only ones. Public health programs are among those that have tapped into capital markets. To fund its vaccination programs, for example, Gavi, the Vaccine Alliance, developed a highly innovative vaccine bond—the International Finance Facility for Immunisation (IFFIm)—that has raised billions of dollars from the capital markets and has to date been credited with immunizing three-quarters of a billion children. Legally binding financial commitments from sovereign states enabled the IFFIm to structure a successful fixed-income product and offer investors a viable investment proposition.[75]

However, many social and environmental programs do not—and may never—meet the profitability requirement. It is hard, for example, to see how domestic violence prevention could become a candidate for a sustainable or impact investment. "Engaging with capital markets is not the right solution all the time," said Charlotte Kaiser, managing director of NatureVest, The Nature Conservancy's investment unit.[76] "The obsession with investing can lead to some bad structures that are not efficient and do not successfully transfer risk. The key question that you need to ask is, 'Is what you are doing addressing a market failure, and hence lends itself to a market solution?'"

Fitness for Impact

Any financing mechanism aiming to benefit society or the planet needs to ensure the money is channeled to the right places at the right time. Insurance programs—such as CCRIF SPC (formerly the Caribbean Catastrophe Risk Insurance Facility), which pioneered multicountry sovereign parametric insurance—have shown the value of insurance as a risk transfer mechanism. In 2017, a decade after CCRIF SPC's creation, it reached a milestone, having paid out just over $100 million to 12 of its 17 member countries, all within 14 days of a disaster (storms, floods, or earthquakes), putting badly needed response funds into the hands of relevant public agencies quickly and efficiently.[77]

However, not all such mechanisms succeed. One that did not meet the "fitness for impact" criterion was the $500 million Pandemic Emergency Financing Facility (PEF), launched by the World Bank in 2017. The PEF, a new model that included the issuance of catastrophe bonds, was developed in the aftermath of the Ebola crisis to give the world's neediest countries access to funding for the next pandemic. The catastrophe bond recently triggered a payment of

$196 million for developing countries to manage the COVID-19 crisis. However, the bond's structure—with payment triggers well into an epidemic as opposed to early on and requiring cases to occur in two countries, including a developing country—meant it was unable to mobilize capital in time to stem the rapid acceleration of the COVID-19 pandemic.

Standardization

Global challenges such as climate change, pandemics, and poverty are extremely complex, have multiple, interrelated causes, cut across national borders, and demand action from public, private, and non-profit sectors. Typically, they also require new, creative solutions and financing mechanisms that can overcome the market failures that have traditionally inhibited investment flows. However, capital markets dislike bespoke mechanisms. They like standardized, easy-to-execute solutions with low transaction costs. To achieve scale, sustainable and impact investment solutions need to be standardized, argues Philippe Zaouati, CEO of asset management firm Mirova. "The projects cannot be small innovative ideas," he said.[78] "While it is exciting to innovate, to make economic sense you also need to make these projects standardized and scalable. We need to figure out how to do that for [new sectors such as] biodiversity."

Lack of standardization has prevented promising social and environmental solutions from attracting larger capital flows. Take social impact bonds, pay-for-performance contracts that raise capital from private investors to fund government social interventions. At one time these pay-for-performance contracts were heralded as mechanisms that could reach scale rapidly, generating what Daniel Stid, of Bridgespan, called "a gold-rush mentality."[79] However, some failed to achieve their goals because the "bonds" were poorly structured; for others, the cost and complexity of putting the deals together and the verification processes meant that they did not offer a universal solution. It's now generally recognized that these financial instruments can provide funding to address certain types of social challenges (such as poor school results or prison recidivism) when there are clear, empirically validated outcomes from which actuaries can construct the instruments. However, the early wave of enthusiasm and rush toward implementation have been followed by disappointment in the mechanism as a broader social financing solution.

Size and Track Record

It's hard to raise institutional capital for new investment products that are sub-scale. Before committing, most institutional investors and wealth platforms want to see a certain size, proven track records, and adequate levels of risk mitigation. This can create hurdles for even the most promising investment propositions.

The challenge is well understood and has motivated philanthropic institutions (such as The Rockefeller Foundation and Omidyar Network), development organizations (such as the Global Environment Facility and the UK's Department for International Development), and high net worth individuals (with more flexible capital) to provide grants and investment capital in support of new investment programs being pioneered by nonprofits.

These include the Forest Resilience Bond (FRB). Developed by Blue Forest Conservation, the FRB's first issuance of $4 million[80] was to implement a forest restoration project protecting 15,000 acres of forestland in Tahoe National Forest, California, using ecologically based methods that reduce the risk of severe fire and protect water resources. It was not large enough to meet the requirements of large institutional players. The relatively small deal instead raised capital from four investors, including two foundations: The Rockefeller Foundation and the Gordon and Betty Moore Foundation. In such situations, early-stage capital support from flexible sources can help promising programs build a track record and grow, improving prospects for attracting institutional capital at a later stage. Having developed a track record through the Tahoe pilot project, the Blue Forest Conservation team is now working to attract more traditional investors to a series of larger-scale projects across US national forests.

How Can Nonprofits Work to Influence Capital Flows?

Even if nonprofits have no assets or programs that could attract investment capital, they can still influence capital flows. Since investors and asset managers are not necessarily experts in areas such as environmental restoration, gender equality, or ethical supply chains, nonprofits can help build market infrastructure, shaping the design of sustainable investment products and enhancing the performance of impact investments. Nonprofits are recognizing that they can be attractive as partners to money managers because of unique assets such as their reputation, their deep understanding of social and environmental challenges, their impact track record, and their on-the-ground networks.

Nonprofits can provide this in a number of ways, whether by publishing papers and guides and spearheading the creation of advocacy-focused coalitions, or by working directly with investors, whether as trusted advisors or through practical partnerships that offer technical assistance.

Research and Thought Leadership

NGO input has proved productive for investors in the extractives sector. For example, in 2016, EDF and the UNPRI published *An Investor's Guide to Methane: Engaging with Oil and Gas Companies to Manage a Rising Risk*. At a time when oil and gas companies were facing growing financial, reputational, and regulatory risks from emissions of methane (a climate pollutant far more powerful than carbon dioxide), the guide helped investors engage with companies in their portfolios to manage risk. The publication covers everything from an introduction to methane and its risks for investors to practical advice on what investors should expect from companies' operational practices, how to ensure their engagements with oil and gas companies on methane are productive, and the kinds of measurement and disclosure they should demand from companies.[81]

Advocacy and Collective Action

As nonprofits have come to recognize the power of investment capital to make an impact—whether positive or negative—on society and the environment, they have helped to form a growing number of coalitions with investors, with the goal of influencing capital flows and increasing the market for sustainable and impact investing. While some coalitions use advocacy to pressure companies to change course, others have been more collaborative, bringing investors and companies to the table to make progress through collective action.

An example of the former is ShareAction, a group pushing for a responsible, transparent investment system that works in the long-term interests of savers, society, and the environment and coordinates shareholder resolutions on issues such as climate change and gender equality. One of its key campaigns, the Living Wage Investor Coalition, coordinates institutional investors—by November 2019 it had 29 members with a total of £2.4 trillion ($3 trillion) in AUM—to press FTSE 100 companies to commit to paying all UK staff and contractors a real living wage. Similarly, the Investor Alliance for Human Rights helps its members (more than 160 institutional investors, with more than $5 trillion in AUM) press companies to advance corporate human rights policies.

A more collaborative coalition is Climate Action 100+. Cofounded by Ceres, it now has 450 investors as members, collectively with more than $40 trillion in AUM, giving it a powerful voice. In addition to playing a leadership role on the steering committee guiding governance and strategy, Ceres also works directly with the coalition's North American companies to reduce their emissions generation, improve their governance, and strengthen their climate-related financial disclosures.

Providing Technical Assistance and Acting as Advisors

Nonprofits can take on the paid role of providing technical assistance to investment funds, as does the technical assistance facility associated with the LDN Fund, mentioned in chapter 5. The technical assistance facility—managed by IDH, the Netherlands-based sustainable trade initiative—helps prepare bankable projects to become viable investment candidates for the LDN Fund and provides postinvestment services to strengthen the impact of the investments.

"We are working very closely with IDH," explained Mirova's Zaouati. "They are playing an instrumental role in helping businesses and projects become investable for the [LDN Fund]. For example, sometimes the project was developed with an NGO model and IDH helped transition to a corporate structure so that it can become investable."

The LDN Fund has also made an investment in a Latin American sustainable land-use program, Urapi. Through the technical assistance facility, IDH provides a number of functions, from improving cooperatives' capacity and strengthening women's leadership to offering support in producing hybrid coffee varieties and ensuring higher climate change resilience. The idea behind the project is to move farmers and their cooperatives away from unsustainable land-use practices that cause deforestation and land degradation and toward commodities such as certified cocoa, coffee, and nuts that can accommodate more sustainable practices.

Development of the fund's framework of environmental and social standards demonstrates how problem solvers (who understand the nature of tangible impact) can work with money managers (who understand finance flows) to come up with innovations in standard setting: Partners in this were the United Nations Convention to Combat Desertification and an advisory group consisting of nonprofits, development institutions, and academia, including the European Investment Bank, WWF, the Rainforest Alliance, and the University of Cambridge.

As investors develop sustainable and impact investing products and funds, well-established nonprofits, such as NGOs and foundations, can become trusted advisors and partners that add credibility to an endeavor. However, nonprofits need to do their own due diligence to ensure they are not simply being used to lend credibility to an investor initiative with no real ability to influence the firm or its products and funds. This means assessing whether sustainable and impact investing is a core ideology for an investor or asset manager or simply a marketing tool. Other considerations include how much control a partner will cede on core developments and impact decisions and how it will make impact versus return trade-offs.

Next Steps

For many problem solvers, working with money managers is not easy. They must make adjustments, build internal capacity, and gain an understanding of the financial sector's workings. So while the next chapter focuses on questions for money managers, problem solvers should not stop reading here. What follows in chapter 7— how money managers can create high-performing sustainable and impact investment programs, how they can help nudge the market, and how the regulatory landscape is shifting—is also relevant to problem solvers. In fact, the better these two groups understand each other, their goals, challenges, and ways of working, the more they can do to accelerate the development of a robust sustainable and impact investing ecosystem.

Chapter 7

The Money Managers

In 2004, former Goldman Sachs partner David Blood and former US vice president Al Gore, together with five other partners, established Generation Investment Management. Their purpose was nothing if not ambitious: to demonstrate the potential of an entirely new form of capitalism. Even so, they felt they needed to seek legal advice to establish whether they could even use sustainability and ESG as part of the firm's fiduciary duty. Fast-forward 16 years: More and more of the firm's clients are asking it to report on impact as well as risk and return. "We believe that impact should be part of your fiduciary duty, because all investing has impact," Blood said.[82]

Back in 2004, Generation's founders believed they could demonstrate the viability of redirecting the financial and business sector's incentives and operations in ways that would dramatically reduce social and environmental damage from unsustainable commercial activities.[83]

"We had a very strong mission to start," Blood said, "which was to prove the business case for this new framework: that sustainable business and investment would lead to more resilient, fair, safe, no carbon, and healthy economies."

The founders also believed they could gain the most traction by focusing on public markets. "First of all, we did have that capability, in that most of the founders were public equity specialists," explained Blood. "But even more so we felt that people identify with public equity markets more than the debt markets, the real estate markets, or private equity markets." And while Generation maintains its commitment to public equities, more than a decade ago it branched out into private equity, closing its third fund in May 2019 raising $1 billion to invest in growth businesses focused on the environment, healthcare, and financial inclusion.

As of December 2019, the firm had more than $25 billion in AUM in both public and private markets. "The good news is there are very strong investment results that we can point to, that our clients can point to," said Blood. "But there's also the academic literature, the trillions of dollars signed up to the Principles for Responsible Investing and the very dynamic entrepreneurs, as well as established CEOs, who've all embraced sustainability over the course of the last three to five years. It's beginning to be considered mainstream, because the business case is clear and robust."

For Generation, the philosophy and framework that guide the firm have changed little since its founding, although the team continues to learn, test, and improve. But as new investment categories have grown, and as more money managers look to integrate sustainable and impact investing into their offerings, the field has become increasingly crowded. The question for newer entrants is how can asset managers maximize the investor's impact return. It's one thing to understand what clients want. It's another to build the kinds of products, portfolios, and strategies that will fit their needs and perform at a high level.

As discussed in chapter 3, asset managers' clients, the asset owners, have changed their focus and demands—something money managers need to understand and support. And as we saw in chapter 5, asset managers also need to establish frameworks and tools for impact measurement. In this and the following chapters, we discuss what else will be critical to their ability to differentiate themselves and to succeed as sustainable and impact investing goes mainstream.

What Policy Frameworks Are Emerging, and What Will Be the Focus for Regulation?

Recent years have seen a rapid rise in sustainability regulation in financial markets. Industry associations such as the GRI (established in 1997), the GIIN (established in 2009), and the Climate Bond Initiative (established in 2009) have long worked to develop principles and guidance for asset owners, asset managers, and intermediaries. But the signing of the Paris Agreement and the adoption of the SDGs in 2015 focused policymakers on the need for financial market transparency and accountability in these areas. Regulators, central banks, and trade associations started crafting rules and frameworks they believed could enable investment capital flows toward sustainable and impact investments while continuing to support market stability and integrity. Of course, regulation varies regionally. However, the general focus for most policymakers is on establishing a taxonomy (or common language) for sustainability and introducing compulsory disclosure requirements to guide capital in the right direction and weed out impact washing and misrepresentation.

The European Approach

The European Union (EU) has been a leader in creating a robust regulatory framework. Introduced in 2018, the European Commission's Action Plan on Financing Sustainable Growth has spurred a number of regulatory initiatives—at various stages of adoption—to support reorienting capital flows toward sustainable investment. These go beyond climate change to areas such as environmental degradation and social issues, as well as the promotion of economic and financial transparency and long-termism.[84] Notable recent regulations include the creation of a taxonomy for sustainable finance and a requirement for EU-based financial market participants to disclose the level of environmental sustainability of their funds and financial products. Where they have none, they must present disclaimers explaining why. They must also include environmental disclosures in regulatory filings.

The commission has also proposed amendments to the EU's benchmarks regulation (governing the financial indices used as benchmarks in financial instruments and contracts). Its view is to create transparency around how index providers build sustainability factors into their calculations and to establish minimum standards for climate benchmarks. The intention is to make it easier for investors to make more informed investment decisions.

The commission is also developing amendments to clarify the sustainability-related roles and responsibilities of asset managers and investment advisors governed by four of its regulatory directives: the Insurance Distribution Directive, the Markets in Financial Instruments Directive (a framework for strengthening investor protection and increasing financial market transparency), the Undertakings for Collective Investment in Transferable Securities Directive (which allows collective investment schemes to operate across the EU), and the Alternative Investment Fund Managers Directive. These include, for example, how to consider sustainability-related risks when assessing investments and how to incorporate sustainability into financial advice to retail investors. Under the proposal, for instance, investment firms and advisors must ask retail investors about their sustainability preferences before offering advice.

Asset owners keen to see capital directed toward sustainable and Paris Agreement–aligned investments have embraced greater regulatory stability and are working to apply it.[85] "If you want to attract long-term investors you have to give them comfort that the regulatory framework is stable and reliable. We are very optimistic about the regulatory initiatives in Europe," said PensionDanmark's Möger Pedersen. Zaouati, CEO of Mirova, sees Europe as a leader in this respect. "The work at the EU level with taxonomy, benchmarks, and reporting is clearly the best we can find all over the world," he said. And because of the global nature of the economy, when the EU regulates, others pay attention. In fact, while the European legislative changes may not apply to all US firms, those that market their funds in the EU will be affected by the new regulation.

Meanwhile, planning to match the ambition of the EU plans, the UK has announced its intention to introduce a series of climate disclosure rules for large listed companies.[86] The rules will initially follow a "comply or explain" requirement. However, in the coming years, they may become mandatory. UK regulators plan to follow up in 2021 with additional rules for other parts of the economy.

The US Approach

It's still unclear whether the SEC will follow Europe's example. For decades, the SEC has considered whether to require registered companies to make sustainability disclosures. Initially, it appeared reluctant to do so. However, in March 2020, the regulator requested input on criteria for funds that have adopted ESG investment strategies. It is exploring how to ensure that what firms tell clients about their ESG strategy matches their actions, and that products claiming to be socially or environmentally responsible actually meet this description. This suggests the SEC is taking the matter seriously. Meanwhile, in May 2020, an SEC Advisory Committee recommendation urged the agency to update its reporting requirements to include ESG factors.[87]

As is often the case in the United States, however, politics influences sustainability-related action. In November 2020, for example, the Trump administration issued a rule to restrict ESG funds in US employer-sponsored retirement plans by requiring them to prioritize economic interests over "non-pecuniary" goals such as ESG.[88] The plan met overwhelming opposition from the mainstream investment community.

Keeping Track of a Changing Landscape

More administrative rulings are likely to emerge in the coming years, and proposals indicate a clear, new direction of regulation, including a streamlining of impact measurement. "Broader European sustainability-related regulations are a good illustration of things that will push the financial system in general to try and coalesce around a common set of analytics," said Hoile, head of asset research at Willis Towers Watson.

What this means for money managers is that they will need to review and update many of their disclosure policies and procedures (to both regulators and investors) and ensure that their regulatory submissions, annual reports, websites, and other disclosures are in compliance—which means building resources internally. More broadly, however, the new regulatory mood enables firms making sustainable and impact investments to distinguish themselves from those investing in polluting, environmentally damaging, or otherwise unsustainable investments. It will also help prevent impact washing, where firms offer so-called sustainable and impact products that in fact have no measurable social or environmental impact.

How Can Money Managers Help Nudge the Market?

As we noted in chapter 2, climate change dominated the agenda at the 2020 Davos meeting of the World Economic Forum. This was perhaps unsurprising, given its increased prominence in the corporate and public consciousness over the previous year. However, what was interesting was the lively debate that emerged over how active asset managers should be in promoting climate action.

"What I say to our clients is: I don't want to be the sharp end of the spear, meaning I don't want to have to be the [one] telling you, or enforcing standards in your industry or in your business," Michael Corbat, Citigroup CEO, told a panel at the event. But while the reality is that money managers must build portfolios according to what their clients want—whether green bonds or the stocks of oil companies—they can help nudge the market toward a more sustainable future in the following ways.

Pioneering Practical Approaches

Players in the financial sector have come together to provide market infrastructure to advance sustainable and impact investing. In 2015, for example, the Financial Stability Board, a global body that monitors and makes recommendations on the international financial system, established the Task Force on Climate-Related Financial Disclosures. The purpose of the TCFD was to develop voluntary, consistent climate-related financial risk disclosures that companies, banks, and investors could use when providing information to their stakeholders.[89] The task force recommendations, published in 2017, have since been piloted in a series of projects with representation from asset owners, asset managers, and intermediaries. In the report published on the projects, all organizations involved agreed on the need for collaboration with peers and policymakers. "The cost of doing nothing is far greater than any costs incurred by taking action," said Maurice Tulloch, then CEO of global insurer Aviva, in the report.[90]

Joining Industry Collaboratives That Guide the Market

In early 2005, then UN secretary-general Kofi Annan invited a group of the world's largest institutional investors to develop what became the United Nations Principles for Responsible Investing. An investor group representing organizations such as Norges Bank Investment Management and PGGM Investments, together with experts from the investment industry, intergovernmental organizations, and civil society, developed a set of principles to guide actions for incorporating sustainability issues into investments. Now including the world's 10 largest asset managers, the UNPRI helps members understand the investment implications of ESG factors and incorporate them into investment decisions. Of course, launching initiatives and becoming signatories to investor initiatives cannot alone move markets. As many are starting to recognize, these initiatives also need to work more actively to ensure that their members and signatories are complying with the principles they have set out.

Sharing Insights with Problem Solvers

Providing feedback to problem solvers on investors' desires is another way money managers can help build the market for sustainable and impact investing. And the most helpful lessons are not always learned from successful investment decisions. Understanding why money managers decide *not* to invest in a product can be equally useful. Fixed-income managers such as Nuveen and Wellington Management believe that sharing what investors care about with issuers is part of their role in helping move the market forward.

"I've worked with an issuer for a year on a transaction to the point where I was helping them write their prospectus language, and the deal came in, it was too rich, so we didn't participate," said Nuveen's Stephen Liberatore. "But we view that time spent as critical because we're trying to elevate the overall market over time." Wellington Management's Campe Goodman stresses how important this kind of feedback is in expanding market engagement. He cites the example of green bond issuances. "We provide feedback on why we invested," he said. "Or why we didn't."

Advising the Regulators

Policymakers are not always financial experts and therefore often seek industry insights when developing regulations. For example, AXA, APG, Deka Investment Group, Aviva Investors, and Mirova are among the organizations represented on the European Commission–led European Union High Level Expert Group on Sustainable Finance. Along with experts from civil society, academia, and other European and international institutions, the 20-member group has provided recommendations for an EU strategy on sustainable finance that integrates Paris Agreement and SDG objectives into Europe's financial system. These will provide the basis for seismic regulatory changes designed to ensure not only that financial markets contribute to sustainable and inclusive growth but also that the system itself is strengthened by addressing risks such as climate change, resource depletion, environmental degradation, and social inequality.

One manager that has enthusiastically engaged in industry conversations about policies and principles is APG Asset Management. "I am a firm believer in partnering with and being party to discussions about our industry's practices and our future. We bring expertise and knowledge that you can only have from being in the trenches," said Claudia Kruse, managing director for global responsible investment and governance at APG. "That is particularly important for understanding unintended consequences." She argues that this is also needed to design principles and policies that can have long-term impact, particularly given the need to look beyond the SDGs and the Paris Agreement, both of which sunset in 2030.

What Can Money Managers Do to Boost Investment Performance—Both Returns and Impact?

The money managers who most successfully integrate sustainability into risk and return goals establish a rigorous method for assessing the sustainability topics on which they engage. This calls for an ability to identify and understand the variables of material importance, which takes on greater urgency when seeking returns in newer and less familiar fields than climate and energy.

Understanding What Matters

As asset managers expand into new sectors, from biodiversity to social and racial justice, they must navigate a complex landscape of unfamiliar issues, making it difficult to determine which elements are most relevant for creating value and managing the risks of their investments. Should a technology company have a social and racial justice policy and goals? Must a consumer and packaged goods firm have pay equity? Should a financial services firm be reducing the greenhouse gas emissions of its physical footprint? While all impact topics may be important for society to address, not all of them create equal financial value—even for investors with very long time horizons.

Moreover, as COVID-19 has revealed, new issues may arise at any time that transform the basis on which judgments about materiality must be made. If some money managers once held a view that infectious diseases and epidemics were only a public health concern, the pandemic has changed that. For those managing investment portfolios, it's now clear that employee safety, public health decisions, and government responses to a crisis can have a direct impact on the corporate bottom line. The pandemic has, for example, resulted in severe credit deterioration for many industries globally, according to S&P Global Ratings.[91]

Assessing materiality is also a challenge for fixed-income investors, who do not have the same rights and engagement opportunities as equity investors. Moreover, the relative prominence of macroeconomic factors such as interest rates, inflation, and safe-haven assets can make it harder to identify which ESG metrics are financially material.

To better understand this, the BlackRock Investment Institute has conducted an analysis of 60 developed and emerging market debt issuers to assess the materiality of ESG in fixed income. Rather than looking at historical data, the institute has taken a forward-looking approach framed by the SDGs to determine material factors. It uses data and indicators from the World Bank's Sovereign ESG Data Portal to calculate impact scores for each. For the E (environmental), it looks at the impact of an issuer's practices and policies on the environment, such as coal-fired power production and annual freshwater withdrawals. For the S (social), it assesses investments in citizens by looking at factors such as access to electricity, school enrollment, and share of seats held by women in national parliaments. And for the G (governance), it looks at the way an issuer is governing its citizens, including factors such as corruption control, government effectiveness, and strength of the rule of law.

The framework uses an equally weighted combination of the three pillar scores to generate an overall score for each country. This is refined by the application of data analytics to a news article search to generate a sentiment score, which highlights developments not captured in the static official data. The research indicates that ESG can explain up to 25% of the variation in emerging market sovereign spreads, which represent the difference in credit quality, and therefore the government's ability to repay. The analysis, which covers 5-year, 10-year, and 30-year bonds, showed that ESG was a stronger indicator of performance than the credit ratings currently provided by ratings agencies.[92]

As we discussed in chapter 5, other firms—such as SSGA and CDC—are developing sophisticated models and tools for assessing materiality. However, money managers will always need to be equipped to make case-by-case evaluations.

Collaborative Engagement

To ensure sustainable and impact investment is delivering intended results, strong and continuing engagement with portfolio companies is essential. Engagement takes many forms, from private conversations to active management, joining forces with other investors or firms to solicit shareholder proposals, and sponsoring research to increase market awareness. Often, it's a combination of these tools.

Because they typically work with management teams on integrating sustainability into an investee's operations, money managers that invest in private equity or private debt have perhaps the most direct engagement with the companies in their portfolios. An example is the investment by LeapFrog Investments, the private equity impact firm, in Kenya's Goodlife Pharmacies.

East Africa's poor health infrastructure and lack of doctors lead half of those needing healthcare to first go to a pharmacy. LeapFrog Investments saw in Goodlife Pharmacies an opportunity for growth and impact and invested tens of millions of dollars. LeapFrog's expert healthcare team worked with management intensively to make the chain's systems and processes scalable. In two years, and in constant collaboration with Goodlife senior management, the firm helped Goodlife's management scale up the chain from 19 to 65 stores in Kenya and Uganda. In addition to the traditional brick-and-mortar stores at malls, the company adopted a modular format that enabled it to set up stores rapidly, even at gas stations. This allowed the company to quickly relocate the stores if they were not economically viable. In conjunction with management, LeapFrog also helped Goodlife convert a number of pharmacies into health hubs with access to telemedicine, nutrition consultations, and laboratory diagnostics, and linked insurers, which cover medication costs.

By 2020, Goodlife was reaching more than 1.5 million people annually and had become the largest healthcare provider in East Africa. "Now you have a better experience at that little gas station than you do in New York and Sydney," said LeapFrog founder and CEO Kuper. "And the value of this company, as you can imagine, has shot through the roof because we're standing with what is now the largest pharmacy group in sub-Saharan Africa outside of South Africa. That is a pretty unique asset."

Goodlife's ability to achieve scale has relied on collaboration between the management team and investors. Michael Jelinske, a LeapFrog vice president who works closely with Goodlife, says he is in touch with Amaan Khalfan, the company's CEO, at least once a week.[93] Khalfan, who was brought on board by LeapFrog to assume the role of CEO, said he has found working with the LeapFrog team to be "extremely enlightening" at the professional level but also finds the relationship productive because of the investment team's ability to test and pilot new ideas and use on-the-ground realities to inform company strategy.[94]

When it comes to public equity investors, forms of ESG and impact engagement typically include activism. While advisory and not legally binding in the United States, shareholder resolutions are often used to make listed companies respond to ESG-related shareholder concerns and priorities, pressing them to adopt more robust sustainability practices, and raising public attention. In 2018, more than two-thirds of shareholder proposals filed at companies in the Russell 3000 Index concerned environmental and social issues.[95] In 2019, Ceres research highlighted some successes of this tool, noting that almost 4 out of 10 climate-related proposals were withdrawn in return for a commitment from companies to address the issues raised by the investors.[96]

However, bowing to pressure in the United States, SEC rules rolled out in 2020 will now significantly limit smaller investors' ability to use shareholder resolutions as a tool. The change is likely to make investors pivot toward newer models and embrace more direct tools of engagement than shareholder proposals. One example of the latter is the Net Zero Asset Owner Alliance, a collaborative of 27 global pension funds and insurers, which by June 2020 had combined assets of $5 trillion. The group is working more directly to influence its portfolio companies to change their business models and adopt climate-friendly practices.

Such collaborative models also appear to be gaining traction as NGOs, managers, and companies come together to experiment with sustainability solutions. One example is the engagement between CDP and Norges Bank Investment Management (NBIM), which manages Norway's Government Pension Fund Global, to work with publicly listed companies in NBIM's equity portfolio on developing strategies to manage and report on risks.

While engagement approaches in public and private equity are well developed, fixed-income investors do not have the same investor rights. "In fixed income, we don't have that vote," said Nuveen's Stephen Liberatore. "But what we do have is the ability to control effectively the purse strings. We can directly invest in target financing. So, we work on trying to structure and focus the deal in such a way that we know we would want to participate."

UNPRI research suggests that such practices are in the early stages of development when it comes to engagement with nation-states, where systematic ESG integration is rarely applied to sovereign debt analysis. Efforts such as those by the BlackRock Institute to define and measure materiality will certainly help create greater understanding and engagement, and we expect to see more collaborations between investors and public officials on developing sustainability principles and tools.

Better Together

In chapter 6 and in this chapter, we looked at the individual challenges facing problem solvers and money managers as they focus on sustainable and impact investment and how each group positions itself to succeed. However, we have seen that as they expand the skills and tools needed to navigate this new landscape, they must equip themselves with a further set of abilities—one that will enable them to collaborate and innovate with new partners. In the next chapter, we look at the challenges that arise when money managers and problem solvers come together, and the steps they can take to ensure the match is a success.

Chapter 8

Making a Match—and Making It Work

L atin America is home to some of the world's largest lakes and rivers. Yet astonishingly, lack of water services means that much of its population is forced to drink contaminated water that causes deadly diseases like cholera. Brazil has a particularly acute problem, with about half the population lacking proper sanitation services and about 15% with no adequate water services. This is just the kind of problem that Wellington Management, an investment management firm with more than $1 trillion in AUM, through its Global Impact Bond strategy, wants to address by investing in investment-grade global fixed-income securities. Many of these are green bonds or social bonds. "But we've identified a lot of opportunities that are not labeled at all," explained Wellington's Campe Goodman.

One such opportunity was a Brazilian water and sanitation company. "One of the analysts came back to me and said, 'We've got the greatest company for you,'" recalled Goodman.

Aside from its credit profile, Wellington saw the company as the kind of problem solver whose impact it could, by making an investment, help scale up. "They are essentially a mission-driven company and yet because they do not issue labeled bonds, most investors in the space do not know about them," explained Goodman. This, he says, is the advantage of working with a large asset management firm like Wellington. "What was exciting about that example was we're covering a lot of these companies already. It's one of the nice things about having the platform of a large organization."

As the Wellington investment illustrates, when money managers find the right match with problem solvers, the combination of monetary assets and social or environmental expertise can advance solutions to seemingly intractable problems. But ensuring that all participants have the same impact goals and agree on the strategies for achieving them is critical. Working across sectors and geographies is not always easy, whether you're a money manager or a problem solver.

If problem solvers, for example, have a culture and operations that prioritize activism and anticapitalist campaigning, they need to decide whether they want to work with an investment firm. Problem-solver companies seeking investments need to ensure their social and environmental returns are real, measurable, and sufficiently valued by their financial partners. And even if they have been working with problem-solver companies for some time, understanding the broader world of problem solvers such as NGOs, activists, and government agencies can be a new challenge for money managers, who may find it perplexing working with problem-solver organizations whose primary driver is not profit.

Money managers may find it hard to conduct due diligence and measure impact with the same rigor as they measure financial return. Meanwhile, problem solvers—who are passionate about the social or environmental impact they know it can make—may be frustrated by the onerous requirements (and, accordingly, time) involved in the diligence process. Yet failure to understand investors' need for due diligence, time lines, and legal commitments can lead to resentment or, worse, a split. Even with the right partners in place, signing an agreement is just the start. The most successful matches occur when money managers and problem solvers build the culture and internal capacity for collaboration between organizations that may have very different ecosystems, risk appetites, and decision-making processes.

How Do Partners Create the Right Ingredients for a Successful Match?

Successful partnering is tough. This means having the right infrastructure in place—from strong leadership to local capacity—which can provide stability during what may be a disruptive exercise for those involved.

Leadership

Commitment to sustainable and impact investing comes from the top. The board of directors (if one exists) and senior leadership must demonstrate a strong, visible, consistent commitment to these investments and establish norms around why they matter. Leadership must also engage early in considering where investment challenges might arise and how colleagues will be asked to manage them.

At APG Asset Management, which manages pension funds on behalf of one in five families in the Netherlands, leadership established three sustainable and responsible investment goals to govern decisions on fixed-income or equity investments: An investment must be able to contribute to financial returns for pension members, must show it takes social responsibility seriously, and—unusually—must contribute to the integrity of financial markets. And instead of shying away from sustainability laggards, APG decided that if potential investments had sufficiently attractive risk, return, and cost criteria, it would work with these companies to improve their sustainability performance.

For example, companies in the palm oil sector can contribute to deforestation—destroying habitats for endangered animals and removing carbon sinks that keep carbon dioxide from entering the atmosphere—and are often known for poor adherence to worker and children's rights. While these are serious issues, palm oil remains a critical source of nutrition and employment and has many useful applications, such as extending product shelf life. Rather than walk away from investing in these companies, APG's leadership decided to engage and deploy a team of specialists locally to work with companies to promote better practices.

Similarly, when problem solvers plan to work with money managers, their leaders need to develop and articulate a clear vision of their organization's impact strategy and of the products and services that are appropriate for investment. They also need to commit to the kinds of business models that allow a company to scale or a project to operate successfully and must be able to create teams that can help them in all this, while remaining open to new ideas as conditions change. In research assessing what problem solvers can learn from business leaders who are integrating sustainability across their strategy and operations, global leadership advisory and search firm Russell Reynolds Associates identified traits such as the ability to think at many levels and to include stakeholders in decisions, a long-term mindset, and the courage to challenge traditional approaches.[97]

Sustained Commitment

Importantly, a demonstrated commitment to impact from each side requires more than just signing up for sustainability consortia. Recent research has concluded that, in aggregate, UNPRI signatories had not shown an improvement in their fund-level ESG scores.[98] So what does an active and sustained commitment look like?

For Amundi, an asset management firm with more than €1.6 trillion in AUM, the journey began in the post–2008 financial crisis period, with its support for an academic center at Columbia University. "We were looking for long-term solutions to the new normal," explained Frédéric Samama, head of responsible investment at Amundi.[99] While research pointed to a need to better understand and manage the ESG risks in client portfolios—particularly climate change—the firm could find no financial products with which to conduct the necessary risk management effectively.

In the search for potential solutions, one of the first steps was a 2011 meeting at The Rockefeller Foundation's Bellagio Center in

Italy, which included a team from Columbia University. At the meeting, Mats Andersson, then CEO of Swedish pension fund AP4, committed to piloting a strategy to decarbonize AP4's equity portfolio. This required developing a financial product that would reduce the pension fund's exposure to companies with a large carbon footprint or exposure to stranded assets, such as fossil fuel reserves at risk of losing value owing to changing demand or new regulations. A subsequent collaboration among Amundi, AP4, MSCI, and France's Fonds de Réserve pour les Retraites (FRR) led to the development of a series of low-carbon indexes and investing strategies—including the Amundi Index Equity Global Low Carbon fund and the Amundi Index Equity Europe Low Carbon fund—for managing and mitigating carbon risk exposure in equity portfolios.

Amundi has since continued its research partnership with Columbia as part of its ongoing thought leadership efforts and product development. And since introducing the first wave of new products to the market, it has mobilized close to €13 billion ($15 billion) in low-carbon index solutions, with about 50% of these tailor-made solutions. It has continued using partnerships to seek out and structure differentiated solutions for other asset classes and geographies. In 2018, working with the IFC, it launched the $1.4 billion Amundi Planet Emerging Green One (EGO) fund, which aims to invest in green bonds issued by emerging markets financial institutions. IFC and Amundi structured the fund to attract institutional investors otherwise hesitant to invest in emerging markets.

For Samama, success begins by involving collaborators in understanding the challenge. "Too often people start with a solution in mind and then start to look for a problem," he said. "You really need to start with a rigorous analytical phase that helps you understand what the obstacles are before you settle on any solutions." In the case of the EGO fund, the obstacle to raising capital from institutional investors was the credit risk of investing in emerging market debt and the challenges of investing in long-term infrastructure projects. "We addressed the first issue by designing a credit-enhancement mechanism to minimize the risk exposure of the institutional investors, and the second by having financial institutions act as the intermediaries who would issue the bonds and then channel the funds to green infrastructure projects," said Samama. While it's too early to assess the strategy's financial and impact performance, the issuance was heavily oversubscribed, proving its effectiveness in attracting institutional investors.

Boots on the Ground

The Nature Conservancy (TNC) has long had a presence in the Central Appalachian coalfields of Kentucky, Tennessee, and Virginia. One of the first communities with which TNC started working was the small town of St. Paul in southwest Virginia. A coal town perched on the edge of the coalfields, St. Paul also happens to sit on the Clinch River, home to one of the highest concentrations of rare and threatened freshwater creatures in North America. "In the mid-nineties, that community contacted TNC and said, 'We really need your help to think about what our future might look like,'" recalled Brad Kreps, director of TNC's Clinch Valley Program, which works to protect 2,200 square miles of mountains and valleys in southwest Virginia and northeast Tennessee.[100] With grant funding, TNC supported a process to help the community with strategic planning that led to the formation of St. Paul Tomorrow, a local community group that developed a plan for sustainable development that focused not only on the river as an asset but also on the surrounding natural areas as potential assets as well.

However, in July 2019, TNC did more: It organized the Cumberland Forest Limited Partnership to acquire 253,000 acres of working forestland in the region by raising capital for a $130 million investment fund from family offices, high net worth individuals, and leading impact investors in natural resources, including some of the clients of Brown Advisory, an independent investment management firm. NatureVest will manage the fund, and, on the land, TNC will implement preservation activities, sustainable timber management, outdoor recreation, solar power projects, and other economic development initiatives that will support local efforts to transition and diversify economies such that they are less dependent on mining.

Investors in the Cumberland Forest Project, as it's known, will receive income through revenues from carbon offset and certified sustainable timber sales, as well as from the sale of the land at the end of the investment period. While preserving natural resources and enhancing community resilience on the land itself, the project also aims to demonstrate that sustainable management of natural assets can deliver returns to investors. "It's basically trying to show that we can make an investment in nature and then we can manage a large property for financial and business outcomes, for conservation outcomes, and also for community benefits," said Kreps. "If we can make Cumberland Forest work, we can take that model and use it to help protect other important places."

The Cumberland Forest Project is an example of the importance of local knowledge when money managers and problem solvers come together. Complex financial instruments to raise and deploy capital for impact may be most successful when all involved have local knowledge, buy-in, and relationships.

For for-profit problem solvers, having local teams is often critical for the goals of many of their money management partners. Kenya-based Twiga Foods is building out a team made up primarily of Kenyans. The company has developed a mobile-commerce platform enabling small urban food retailers to source directly from farmers and food manufacturers, lowering the cost of food and increasing incomes for local farmers and producers. Its platform supports 18,000 retailers and 5,000 to 6,000 orders a day. Cofounder Grant Brooke argues it is simply "better business practice" to build a team whose members are designing products and services for their "aunts and uncles" as opposed to bringing in expats who need to familiarize themselves with culture and context.[101] Many investors see community engagement—via physical presence, local team building, and other means—as essential for any impact-focused enterprise or investment.

More money managers are also creating a local presence to facilitate deeper engagement with their investments. Having "boots on the ground" was, for example, one of the reasons that, in 2017, PensionDanmark invested in AP Moller Capital's first infrastructure fund, the New Africa Infrastructure Fund, which was designed to support sustainable development and improvements in living standards across the continent. What attracted PensionDanmark to the investment was, as CEO Möger Pedersen put it at the time, AP Moller Capital's "extensive local investment experience combined with a strong network and a promising pipeline of potential investment projects."

What Does Making a Successful Match Mean for a Problem-Solver Organization's Internal Capacity?

When working with money managers, problem solvers must think about the organizational capacity needed to build a strong partnership. This often means adding financial and human resources and changing procedures in areas such as communications and impact measurement.

Structure and Resources

For problem solvers, the structural elements underpinning a successful match need to be not only embedded in their organization's strategy but also reflected in how they marshal their resources—both financial and human. When it comes to direct investment propositions, one option is to set up a dedicated unit to focus on sustainable and impact investment opportunities. For example, in 2014, four years after TNC created an impact capital strategy, it launched NatureVest to source and structure investment products that support TNC's mission. The decision to launch a dedicated unit came after testing the market and getting investor feedback. "We are an entrepreneurial place, so there was great excitement for the strategy," recalled NatureVest's Kaiser. "There was a realization that across the organization, opportunities existed—like fish quota acquisition, working land acquisition, and green infrastructure in cities—that could be financed differently."

Another approach, by a problem-solver company, is that of Novozymes, a Danish biotech company. It set up an internal Sustainability Development Board as a means of integrating sustainability into its day-to-day operations. Heads of departments from procurement to R&D and marketing are all required to sit on the board and to present sustainability challenges from their functional areas, along with goals and strategies for meeting them. This engages the entire business in the corporate sustainability effort and makes it easier to identify related risks and opportunities.

Impact Measurement

Sometimes, surprisingly, problem solvers lack the capacity to develop or use the impact assessment frameworks of their capital sector partners. From the outset, ensuring these skills are present internally or affordable through external consultants is essential, especially since investors expect an analytic rigor that is different from what most philanthropic or charitable funders expect. As the sector evolves, some impact investors are more amenable to allowing their portfolio companies to identify the impact metrics most important to their core business. This is particularly important for companies operating across sectors, making it difficult to capture data through a specific impact-tracking methodology.

One example is SunCulture, a manufacturer and distributor of products that improve productivity for smallholder farmers in Africa. Initially known for solar-powered irrigation technology, SunCulture has since expanded into making, selling, and financing a variety of solar products, enabling it to attract investors from the consumer, solar, and agriculture sectors. Samir Ibrahim, CEO and cofounder, notes that investors have become more aware that the problems SunCulture is solving are systemic and don't fit neatly into any given sector. "Seven or eight years ago, impact investors were looking at impact in a very specific way, and they've broadened the way that they look at impact. That makes it easier to raise money," he said.[102]

Of course, this means problem solvers must be able to tell a compelling story about which metrics matter to them and why, allowing for collaborative identification of impact metrics that reflect both the scale of the business and its impact.

Financial Planning and Skills

Engaging with the capital markets requires financial acumen. For those with sufficient resources, skills can be acquired through recruitment. Others must develop them internally—and the learning curve can be steep. However, if an organization plans to put investors' capital at risk with the promise of financial reward, it is essential to have people with skills and experience in capital markets who can speak the investment community's language.

At The Rockefeller Foundation, as we built our impact investing and financial innovation program, we knew we needed a unit of people experienced in working with and in capital markets. We reequipped and reorganized to be able to source and structure investment products in collaboration with financial industry partners. That meant recruiting people with backgrounds in strategy and experience in multiple, relevant domains of the finance and investment management industry, such as private equity, community development finance, guarantee programs, and fixed income.

Internal structures, budgets, and processes that enable new, relevant forms of capital to flow easily will be taken into account by investors in their due diligence. And since capital market instruments require long-term and legally binding financial commitments, problem solvers should build relevant legal capacity into their budgets and operations, as these agreements are often complex.

What Does Making a Successful Match Mean for a Money Manager's Internal Organization?

As is the case for problem solvers, money managers also need to create the right internal resources. They need new forms of expertise, nontraditional incentive structures, and a culture that enables sustainable and impact investing approaches to be integrated throughout the organization.

Talent and Skills

Perhaps most important are people with skills specific to impact and sustainability. Are investment managers, for example, equipped to distinguish a company that is genuinely working toward environmental sustainability from one that simply has a good PR machine? Are they able to offer investment products and portfolios that are customized rather than standardized? Not all firms possess these capabilities. And if they do, people who understand and are committed to impact may not reside in every part of the business. New roles are often needed, such as data scientists and experts with deep understanding of social and environmental factors. And, as impact and finance sector talent pools merge, money managers need to build hybrid capabilities—impact, policy, and finance.

While many organizations may already have sustainability teams, they often need to revamp from a modestly staffed, ESG-compliance-focused unit to one capable of developing sophisticated impact investment strategies, products, and evaluation methodologies. Moreover, embedding sustainable and impact investing approaches across a firm means training existing employees, such as portfolio managers and risk managers, to use sustainability and ESG data and analytics as value-creation and assessment tools. Firms with this goal typically expand their research and thought leadership capabilities to include experts capable of generating insights on key sustainability topics that demonstrate to clients that the firm is able to increase value.

Incentives

In some cases, the barrier for a firm is an incentive structure that is not aligned with the belief of sustainable and impact investing as a value-creation tool. A firm may encounter resistance when embracing a strategy that represents a significant departure from how money managers operate. Heads of municipal finance, for example, might question why they need to do things differently when they have no problem placing debt in traditional bond markets and getting paid for it. It's therefore important for firms to create incentives for staff to work to generate impact.

Embracing different time frames may also be challenging. "You need longer time horizons to be assured that your good work will crystallize good outcomes," said Roger Urwin, co-head of Willis Towers Watson's Thinking Ahead Institute.[103] "But it's not easy to resist the one-to-three-year performance challenge that will come up on a sustainability oriented portfolio, which you may not have the collateral to defend yourself against."

Kenneth Lay, senior managing director at Rock Creek Group and former treasurer of the World Bank, argues that when it comes to ESG, firms need to figure out how to reward managers for taking a long view. "The underlying incentive model that backs it all—a salary plus an annual bonus based heavily on shorter-term market indicators—is going to have to change," said Lay.[104] "The notion that an asset management firm managing money for people with a 10-to-20-year investment horizon is rewarding its people with annual bonuses—there is a certain inconsistency there."

GPIF—which has stated that compensation structures should reflect managers' philosophy as well as their values and beliefs—commissioned human resources consulting firm Mercer to survey its asset managers to understand whether their firms had schemes in place to discourage short-termism and promote long-termism and stewardship. It found that leading companies designed their compensation strategies to increase long-term returns (whether stipulated or communicated), assessed mid- to long-term investment performance, and evaluated teamwork and contributions to organizational and talent development. However, few managers provided information or had strong structures for aligning the compensation of their head of ESG with the ESG performance of their portfolio.[105]

Culture

Some see full acceptance of sustainable and impact investing as part of an asset management company's practice as requiring a fundamental cultural shift. Claudia Kruse describes APG's journey from 2007, when it hired its first responsible investment professional, to today as a "cultural transformation, where we have learned to think in sustainability terms across the organization." To enable this transformation, she adds, commitment must come from the top, and the sustainability agenda should be integrated across the enterprise. "That is key as we do not just have a pocket of the portfolio where we look for sustainability but it really has to apply everywhere—in the way we invest and conduct our business."

Norihiro Takahashi, former CEO of GPIF, understood the need to embed sustainability thinking throughout the organization and to shift its culture. Under his leadership, the pension fund aligned its strategy to build reserves and generate returns that could match the challenges of Japan's aging society. Takahashi's sharp focus on creating long-term value for the Japanese economy was the reason sustainability became a core consideration for all GPIF's investment strategies. Before retiring, he shared his thoughts in an interview with IPE on implementing the strategy shift. "ESG now drives our investment principles. It forms the basis of our investment decisions. I expect our staff to be concerned and mindful of environmental issues; that they have a curiosity about social problems in the world," he said.[106]

What Big Challenges Remain to Be Resolved Between Problem Solvers and Money Managers?

When they come together to advance sustainable and impact investing, problem solvers and money managers need to accept their differences, define shared goals, and find ways of meeting in the middle. But some challenges remain.

Value Versus Values

For the growing number of money managers engaging in sustainable and impact investing, the focus is a value-driven imperative, not a values-driven agenda. For example, investments in areas such as climate action, human capital management, or supply chain resiliency tend to be based first on how these factors affect financial performance rather than primarily on a mission to protect the planet or prevent human rights abuses. By contrast, the latter may be the primary driver for problem solvers, particularly for nonprofits. These differences in motivation should not, however, prevent engagement. Instead, they should be accommodated in the way partnerships are structured.

This requires discussion between partners up front. This was the case when one organization strongly driven by its values entered a partnership with an organization driven by value. In 2017, UNICEF Norway approached the $1 trillion Government Pension Fund Global of Norway, managed by Norges Bank Investment Management (NBIM). The agency was interested in advancing global corporate policies and practices to strengthen children's rights in the apparel and footwear industry, which UNICEF estimates affects the lives of more than 100 million children worldwide, as employees, as the children of employees, or as members of the communities around factories and farms.

For NBIM, protecting children's rights has been a corporate engagement priority across all its investments since 2008. NBIM sees it as part of strong business practice and effective risk management.

As a result, the two organizations decided to explore a new collaboration model.

Leveraging NBIM's voice as an influential global shareholder and UNICEF's deep expertise on children's welfare, the partners convened a new network selected from NBIM's portfolio of companies—including the largest European sportswear manufacturer Adidas, Swedish fashion retailer H&M, Gucci owner Kering, and the VF Corporation. It was designed to deepen understanding of industry challenges and improve the policies and practices governing the rights of children, not just as workers but also as members of the global supply chain.

In June 2020, NBIM and UNICEF published a report on children's rights in the garment and footwear industries, as well as a guide for companies on how to uphold them. Over time, this guidance is expected to influence business policies and practices across sectors and become embedded in both legal frameworks and the investment policies of global asset management firms. For NBIM, the partnership has been an opportunity to further develop its own policies. "Reflecting some of the discussions in the network, we updated our public company expectations on children's rights in 2019, emphasizing the importance for children's rights of decent working conditions for young workers, parents and careers," wrote Carine Smith Ihenacho, NBIM's chief corporate governance officer, in the report.[107]

The Fungibility of Money

Unlike money managers, nonprofits need to attribute impact to all of their capital. However, investment managers often carry investments in their portfolios that are not sustainably invested. This may lead problem solvers and others to look with skepticism at money managers' claims about their focus on ESG, such as in some emerging criticism of BlackRock. "Larry Fink has a lot to say about his firm's climate credentials but next to nothing to show for it," Brynn O'Brien, executive director at the Australasian Centre for Corporate Responsibility, was quoted in the *Financial Times* as saying.[108]

As with the "value versus values" debates, this means that problem solvers choosing to engage must be willing to accept that few money managers will be "100% impact," at least in the short to mid term. In addition, they should be philosophically willing and technically able to evaluate the level of impact a partnership will yield, relative to the risks associated with engaging.

Profit Versus Impact

Consensus is increasing among money managers and problem solvers that in the long term, financial returns and impact do not involve trade-offs. However, this consensus could be weakened if money managers push problem-solving entrepreneurs to satisfy increasingly high returns expectations in the short term—particularly if economic conditions shift.

At Goodlife Pharmacies, for example, CEO Khalfan says impact becomes an even more fundamental concern during times of macroeconomic instability. For a company like Goodlife, which has not only captured the affluent and middle-class markets but is also establishing itself as a core provider of care to low- and middle-income markets, macroeconomic destabilization can have a negative impact on the business. This leads to many challenges, including maintaining employment while also creating a sustainable business. Khalfan argues, however, that to navigate such dilemmas it is essential to set clear expectations and identify priorities with investors from the outset, and to continue engaging with these issues, even in times of turbulence. In this respect, he adds, "LeapFrog has been a fantastic partner."

Divergence on Time Horizons

Money managers and problem solvers (whether nonprofits, philanthropists, or governments) do not necessarily share the same time line when it comes to addressing social and environmental problems. They may agree on the urgent need to act. But their time lines for outcomes may diverge. Also one of the biggest challenges for problem solvers seeking direct investment—particularly those of smaller ticket sizes—is the sluggish speed of the diligence and investment processes.

SunCulture's Ibrahim found that it takes significantly longer to raise money from impact investors than it does from, say, strategic investors or more traditional venture capitalists. The problem, he says, is that when investors conduct a 12-month fund-raising process, they are asking questions today that may not matter in a year's time, because things change so fast. This can be frustrating for entrepreneurial problem solvers with ideas they want to scale up rapidly. "It goes against what needs to happen in this market, in terms of speed and the ability to figure out what's going to work and what's not going to work. The faster we know what works and what's not going to work, the better it is for everybody."

The Benefits of the Collaborative Spirit

As the sustainable and impact investing sector matures, participants are learning how to work together more effectively. Problem solvers are becoming increasingly financially savvy, often raising mission-critical funds from private investors by creating new kinds of financial instruments that access the capital markets, as TNC has done. And companies created to deliver social or environmental products or services, such as SunCulture, Cellulant, Twiga Foods, and Goodlife Pharmacies, are attracting significant investment capital. Meanwhile, money managers are becoming increasingly comfortable partnering with problem solvers (even former adversaries that once campaigned against them) as they develop more sustainable and impact investing products and strategies.

And while, as this chapter highlights, significant challenges can emerge when bringing these actors together, with their different objectives, time lines, and ways of working, these very differences often add an essential ingredient to the mix: diversity. In fact, as more and more research is demonstrating, diversity is key to innovation. In the next, final chapter, we'll show how break-through innovations create stepping-stones that will enable the world of finance to become an even more effective catalyst for the large-scale transformations needed to move to a more sustainable, equitable world.

PART III

The Future

Chapter 9

The Innovation Imperative

G rowing in temperate climates, *taraxacum officinale*—the common dandelion—is a plant some consider a weed, others a medical herb. It is an ingredient in pesto, soup, jelly, and even wine. It provides nectar for insects, and its leaves and seeds feed birds and animals. When it sheds its brilliant yellow flowers, it makes way for delicate white globes that, as hundreds of seeds are dispersed in the wind, begin new life. But could it be an investable asset?

The answer, according to the Intrinsic Value Exchange, is yes. Launched in 2013, IVE is a mission-driven enterprise that aims to convert natural assets—such as dandelions, coral reefs, and alpine forests—into financial capital, addressing what IVE argues is the failure of current economic systems to place a monetary value on many life-sustaining natural, human, and social domains. This has become increasingly urgent with the awareness that biodiversity and a healthy natural infrastructure are vital to human health and a thriving economy. IVE's goal is to create a financial mechanism to protect, restore, and expand natural areas. To enable the financial value of natural assets to be monetized, IVE is working with natural asset owners such as governments to structure these assets into tradable companies that will hold the right and responsibility for managing the productivity of the assets. IVE will then assist the owners of these companies in taking them public on exchanges, such as the New York Stock Exchange. The fledgling enterprise is currently collaborating with Costa Rica and other governments to pioneer the Natural Asset Company structure.

This is not a novel idea. It is based on a model that goes back centuries. In 1602, the Dutch East India Company offered shares in its business to the general public, effectively conducting the world's first initial public offering and setting in motion a mechanism that has led to the daily trading of many trillions of shares in public companies around the world. IVE's use of this mechanism is, however, an innovation that uses an old idea in a compelling new way.

This is why, in 2015, we created The Rockefeller Foundation's Zero Gap initiative. We wanted to search the world for breakthrough innovations that would offer new ways to use capital markets for a more sustainable world, and to provide grants and program-related investments to seed pilot work and development, whether by building new investment markets or making existing markets more accessible. In IVE, one of the recipients, we saw great potential to effect systems change by creating mechanisms and structures that value nature in a different way—turning ecosystems into an investable productive asset that can become part of the economic mainstream.

In another case, Zero Gap funding enabled a critical feasibility study. In 2015, Africa GreenCo (AGC) was just an idea—an intriguing one—for changing the energy investment business model in sub-Saharan Africa. Its concept note set out a vision for a new type of institution for Africa, a public-private partnership that would create a creditworthy entity to act as a risk-mitigating intermediary for power projects, playing a potentially transformational role in bringing in private investments to the sector.

It was certainly ambitious, aiming to fill a very big gap: Sub-Saharan Africa is home to 14% of the world's population, yet only half its citizens have access to electricity. And where there is power, households, businesses, and communities pay high prices for poor service. In 2018, for example, 80% of sub-Saharan African companies suffered frequent electricity disruptions, leading to economic losses. By some estimates, such disruptions cost the region up to 5%

of GDP annually, hampering sustainable economic growth, job creation, poverty reduction, and inward investment flows. With the continent's population expected to double by 2050, the challenge of limited and unreliable energy access will only be exacerbated.[109]

Part of the problem is the weak financial position of the region's utilities and the limited options of alternative buyers when utilities are unable to pay. This has long deterred private investors from investing at scale, either for energy transmission and distribution or for expanded power generation. AGC aimed to tackle this by improving the risk profile of the region's investments. It would purchase power from independent power projects (IPPs) across the Southern African Development Community region through power purchase agreements, then sell that power to a diversified portfolio of purchasers (mostly utilities, but also private buyers) through power supply agreements. It would mitigate the risk of purchaser default by securing alternative buyers through trading on the South African Power Pool electricity markets.

Today, it's impressive to see how far AGC has come. In the past few years, it has raised funds from development finance institutions and has received widespread recognition. For example, it was selected as one of the Scale-Up Partnerships run by P4G (Partnering for Green Growth and the Global Goals 2030), a global forum for developing public-private partnerships working to meet the SDGs and the Paris Agreement. This year, in partnership with the government, it will begin operations in Zambia by setting up a jointly owned, but independently managed, creditworthy intermediary electricity "off-taker." AGC then plans to replicate the model across Africa.

Another area ripe for innovation is expanding access to sustainable and impact investments for individual investors. Currently, few investment products allow them broad access to such investments. Project Snowball aims to change this, with the goal of democratizing and diversifying the impact investment community.

Started in 2016 as a partnership among several UK charitable trusts—including one linked to the 350-year-old privately owned bank C. Hoare & Co.—Snowball is building a one-stop-shop investment product for individuals who want to make double-bottom-line investments but cannot currently access or build such portfolios on their own. It is creating a diversified vehicle that will invest in multiple asset classes (such as fixed income, public equities, real estate, and private equity) and multiple sectors (such as housing and communities, education and employment, financial inclusion, and social justice).

As of May 2020, Snowball had built up a portfolio of investments including Civitas Social Housing, the Renewables Infrastructure Group, Greencoat Renewables, Bluefield Solar, Lyme Timber, Affordable Homes Rental Fund, and National Homeless Property Fund. Once it reaches a critical threshold of AUM, it plans to launch a publicly listed, closed-end investment vehicle on the London Stock Exchange.

Another innovation committed to greater diversity—in this case in the venture capital world—was launched in 2015. Portfolia's goal is to enable women to flex their financial muscles by backing the entrepreneurial teams and types of goods and services they want to see in the world, for returns and impact. Cited as game changing for women investors, it was chosen by *Fast Company* in 2020 as one of the world's most innovative companies. Portfolia also represents a disruptive venture investing model, selecting five substance experts to lead each fund, and inviting all qualified investors (who are required to make a minimum investment of $10,000 per fund) to participate when the entrepreneurs "pitch" their companies and in the due diligence process. The idea, says the company, is to create for women investors an investing experience that is "transparent, collaborative, educational and enjoyable."[110]

The Growth Trajectory

Project Snowball, Portfolia, AGC, and IVE seek more than incremental change. Their founders have come up with ideas that address market failures and expand the reach of capital markets in new ways. So what is required besides the innovators themselves to foster new ideas?

Taking the Politics Out of Investing

Unfortunately, when it comes to investing to mitigate social and environmental challenges, politics often gets in the way. As many asset managers have told us, when issues such as climate change, gender discrimination, and inequality, as well as business practices and capitalism, are framed as a debate about "values and ideologies," it obscures the fact that environmental, social, and governance factors have a material impact on the financial return of investments.

For this reason, the importance of the move of the world's largest asset owners—such as Japan's GPIF—into sustainable and impact investing goes beyond the dollars they are unleashing for impact. These investors can legitimize the argument for using ESG and impact as a lens for investment decisions—not because of their values but because it is their fiduciary duty to deliver superior risk-adjusted returns.

Risk Capital for Innovation

An ongoing innovation pool needs to be created to fund early-stage R&D—resources that should be accessible by the entire industry, from asset owners and asset managers to nonprofits and government agencies. Often these capital pools for early-stage innovation have been provided by foundations that are willing to fund the highest-risk phase of piloting new investment structures and to provide leverage for raising larger and more commercial sources of capital. An example is the development of Apeel Sciences (mentioned in chapter 4). While it subsequently attracted investors such as DBL Partners, Apeel Sciences was founded and grown with a grant from the Bill & Melinda Gates Foundation. Though philanthropy has a critical role to play, government support is needed for this kind of agile innovation capital at scale. A great model is the successful US Defense Advanced Research Projects Agency (DARPA), which among other things developed the ARPANET, precursor to the internet.

A Pathway to Scale

Innovation is hard and often involves failure and repeated attempts. Innovators need not just funds to test pilots but also sufficient resources and support to grow their enterprises and scale up proven solutions sufficiently before they become attractive to capital markets. Again, philanthropy must play a larger role and so must development finance institutions. While green bonds now attract large sums of capital markets' money for climate-related projects, the World Bank and regional development finance institutions acted as a catalyst for their launch and promotion and enabled the growth of the market. As early as 2007, the European Investment Bank issued a climate awareness bond, its first. The €600 million ($675 million) equity-index-linked bond's funds were used to finance renewable energy and energy efficiency projects. And a year later, the World Bank issued the world's first labeled green bond. What the development finance institutions started, investors have now embraced with enthusiasm. These kinds of support mechanisms are essential to enable entrepreneurs and innovators to turn audacious ideas into investment offerings and partnerships.

Asset Owners on the Leadership Stage

Finally, a greater number of asset owners need to be seen as publicly leading the agenda. Since they are instrumental in shaping capital markets, their leadership is critical. With considerable assets and credibility, they must assume the role of heavyweights on the public stage, more directly prompting others to act. And while some have started building their own sustainable and impact investing expertise and leadership capacity—from management to the board—they should continue this process and encourage peers to follow. After all, asset owners' demands provide the most powerful incentive for asset managers to change behavior; and when asset managers visibly show that they are looking for new options, they create demand for the kinds of innovative enterprises featured in this chapter.

Shifting Capitalism's Trajectory

As we look at the bold, ambitious work of the innovators featured here and others, we find plenty of reasons for optimism. What's exciting is that the innovations on the horizon are building on the ideas, products, and partnerships we reviewed in earlier chapters. They will provide access for new types of investors, form new kinds of marketplaces linking different sources of capital, and develop new types of investments in society, whether that's protecting the true value of assets such as forests or agricultural land or creating mitigation offsets that help conserve water and biodiversity. And they come at a time when more and more investors—recognizing the risks to their portfolios from inequality, climate change, pollution, and the loss of the earth's nutrients, species, and biodiversity—are hungry for new investment options.

Not all these innovators will be able to scale up their ideas. But more will follow. And those who succeed will help put further trillions of global capital markets dollars to work for society and the environment. Innovation is at the heart of efforts to shake up the old ways of investing and pave the way for new forms of capitalism that can bring about transformational impact for the health of people and the planet.

Epilogue

Since we began writing this book, the world has changed. The COVID-19 pandemic has cost hundreds of thousands of lives and destroyed countless livelihoods. Governments have thrown out the rulebook on spending. Companies have made their operations virtual and rethought core business models. Environmentalists speculate on whether the pandemic might turbo-charge or hinder climate action. Individuals question everything from how and why they travel to their spending patterns. And, of course, the crisis has had serious short-term and long-term implications for the capital markets. Meanwhile, with a rise in social- and racial-justice demonstrations across parts of the globe, the issue of human rights seems to have finally broken through in the corporate world, bringing attention to not just societal ills but also their damaging effect on the economy and, by extension, investments.

These developments have significant implications for sustainable and impact investing. But how will they play out? We see two key trends ahead. First, sustainable and impact investing will continue to gain momentum. Second, all three elements of ESG—particularly the S—will undergo a transformation. And, added to ESG, the spotlight will fall on resilience as a fourth metric, as rebuilding efforts focus on creating economies less vulnerable to shocks and as investors seek companies that are prepared for the next crisis.

Sustainable and Impact Investing's Momentum Will Grow

Investor attention on sustainable and impact investing has actually risen during the COVID-19 crisis. Part of this was driven by the crisis itself. For example, investor demand increased significantly for investment products addressing the effects of the pandemic on society, such as COVID-19 bonds issued by public agencies, banks, and corporates. Among the most notable initiatives was the European Union's plan to finance the bloc's COVID-19 €750 billion recovery package with social and green bonds issued by the European Commission. Another was Bank of America's billion-dollar corporate bond, issued to provide financing to the health industry. Meanwhile, ESG funds outperformed traditional ones and, between April and June 2020, received inflows of more than $71.1 billion globally.

Investors clearly see a strong ESG focus as a proxy for good corporate management, something investors have traditionally rewarded. And while not all ESG funds will deliver the same level of returns, their robust performance during much of 2020 has largely put to rest the argument that focusing on sustainability means sacrificing financial reward. In the process, the three elements of ESG are expanding and becoming more clearly defined.

The *E* in ESG

Given the profound questions it has raised about the way we live, COVID-19 will lead to a broadening of interpretations of the *E* in ESG. First, the highly infectious nature of the virus has prompted rapid changes in the way we shop, work, and travel, all of which are critical in tackling climate change. Within weeks, for example, with little time to prepare, much of the corporate world was working virtually. This raised questions about whether other similarly drastic changes in corporate activity—previously thought too difficult or expensive—could be made to prevent unsustainable resource consumption and avert a climate crisis.

The pandemic has also further raised awareness of the interconnectedness among the economy, human health, the climate, and natural ecosystems. This has led many investors to conclude that environmental considerations must go beyond cutting greenhouse gas emissions to other elements such as biodiversity and natural resources, which if neglected can have a profound impact on the health of communities and essential food and water supplies. A 2020 research report by the World Economic Forum estimates that more than half of global GDP is exposed to risks from loss of nature.[111] Modeled after the influential Task Force on Climate-Related Financial Disclosure, the recently launched Task Force for Nature-Related Financial Disclosure—which seeks to create voluntary and consistent financial risk information for businesses to give to their investors, insurers, and other stakeholders—is a clear step toward expanding the *E*.

The *S* in ESG

In the wake of the COVID-19 pandemic, social issues assumed new prominence. First, the pandemic highlighted the fact that lack of social protections and robust public health approaches damages economies. This has prompted investors to apply greater scrutiny to the way companies plan to protect the health and safety of workers against the effects of future crises. Also in 2020, the Black Lives Matter movement raised awareness of the need for an expanded approach to diversity and inclusion in the corporate world. In short, the human, social (*S*) side of corporate performance has risen sharply up the ESG agenda.

The crisis has led to an understanding among more investors that poor treatment of employees, suppliers, and contractors, human rights abuses, and failure to address social justice not only are morally offensive but also create material risks to businesses and, by extension, to their investments. As a result, more investors will focus on how companies are promoting inclusion and human rights. The UNPRI recently announced a plan for its 3,110 signatories to incorporate human rights into their investments.[112]

The focus goes beyond diversity in hiring practices, flexible work schedules or working from home, paid sick leave, and better health benefits. Investors will be increasingly interested in whether companies are building the inclusive, equitable workplaces that give them the "social license to operate" (public or stakeholder acceptance for commercial operations). Talk of a social license to operate is not new. But while it once applied to the way companies treated factory workers in developing countries or the communities around their mining operations, the effect of the pandemic has been to expand the concept to how companies broadly protect their stakeholders.

The G in ESG

Corporate governance assessment primarily focuses on issues such as transparency, tax strategies, and business codes of conduct, along with management of compliance and risk. However, as with the E and S in ESG, the concept of governance is now likely to be extended beyond these boundaries. Even small governance changes demonstrating greater accountability across all areas of a business could be significant.

Meanwhile, new elements of governance are rising up the agenda, particularly leadership, which in this period of transformation is becoming a critical element of the G in ESG. There is an increased focus on assessing the degree to which the board and CEO are capable of integrating sustainability into business strategies and implementing it across their operations, holding the C-suite and managers accountable in measurable ways. A recent Russell Reynolds study highlighted this as an area where many corporates currently fall short. While 92% of CEOs responding saw integration of sustainability as critical to business success, only 48% said that they were implementing sustainability in their operations.[113] Leadership teams will also be judged by how well they include stakeholders in relevant decisions, adopt a long-term sustainability mindset, and challenge traditional approaches when necessary.

A more robust definition of the G will require business leaders to step up, both as leaders of their organizations and collectively with industry peers, to advance a more material and effective sustainability agenda.

ESGR: Adding Resilience

COVID-19 has warned us that more crises with devastating human and economic consequences could be around the corner. This makes the need to build capacity to prepare more effectively, rebound more quickly, and even achieve transformation more urgent. Resilience is rapidly making its way into corporate and investment conversations. We believe this calls for introducing a new element to risk-return calculations, investment due diligence, and sustainability metrics through the addition of the letter R to ESG.

Our work has shown that resilience rests on five critical pillars that are buildable and measurable. Resilient companies have the following:

- Willingness and ability to assess and absorb new information and adjust quickly using monitoring and feedback loops
- Diverse and redundant backups and supply chain alternatives to access if one part of the system is challenged
- Seamless information sharing, decision-making, and transparent communication that ensures coordinated action across their entire operations
- Strong self-regulating capabilities, so failure in one part of the system can be delinked, preventing its spread and permitting safe rather than catastrophic failure
- An ability to be nimble and adjust quickly to changing circumstances by developing new plans and taking new actions

Everything from energy security and supply chain redundancies to the viability of local transportation systems, nimble and integrated work teams, and ready access to real-time data will become more important to investors. Building more successful portfolios will therefore involve not only using more robust ESG factors but also measuring the nature and strength of a company's resilience.

We are aware, of course, that this is a field already weighed down by abbreviations. Nevertheless, given that crisis is the new normal, we argue strongly for making ESGR a new lens through which to view sustainable and impact investments. With resilience considerations embedded in investment decisions, we believe the financial sector will be far better positioned to act as a catalyst for the creation of a world that is safer, stronger, more equitable, and more environmentally sustainable—in short, the kind of world in which we all want to live.

Acknowledgments

First, we are grateful to our many colleagues at The Rockefeller Foundation while we were in leadership roles there, and to the broad, global impact investing and sustainable finance community whose brilliant work inspired us to write this book. From our early efforts, in which we promoted and expanded the idea that purpose and profit can work together to produce extraordinary impact, we had a clear-eyed vision that a new way of investing was key. We are grateful to the many partners along the way, from pioneering asset owners and money managers, to the entrepreneurs, company leaders, and risk-taking nonprofits that showed that this was possible. We interviewed and featured many of them in this book, and they are acknowledged below. We especially want to salute the grantees of The Rockefeller Foundation Zero Gap program for their expertise, creativity, and commitment, and we thank The Rockefeller Foundation for the research grant that facilitated our work.

We owe deep gratitude to Sarah Murray for serving as senior editor for this work. She has been a spectacular partner. Our equally sincere thanks to Ellen Halle and Melanie Kinard for their research and interviewing assistance. Collectively, their hard work was instrumental in gathering the stories that we share in this book.

To the publishing team at Wharton School Press who helped take this book from initial concept to reality—Shannon Berning and Brett LoGiurato, we thank you.

Many experts and innovators working on the cutting edge of sustainable and impact investing shared their perspectives and stories with us. To the following people, and their colleagues and institutions, we offer our thanks for the time and wisdom you shared with us: Torben Möger Pedersen, Jan Kæraa Rasmussen, Frédéric

Samama, Claudia Kruse, Liesel Pritzker Simmons, Michael Hankin, Ken Njoroge, Divine Muragijimana, Andrew Dawber, Jessie Woolley-Wilson, Dave Chen, Vivek Subramanian, Nithya Balakrishnan, David Blood, Amit Bouri, Amaan Nizaar Khalfan, Naori Honda, Stanley Bergman, Hans Peter Lankes, Dr. Andrew Kuper, Michael Jelinske, Philippe Zaouati, Gautier Quéru, Charlotte Kaiser, Stephen Liberatore, Jay Reinemann, Kenneth Lay, Colin Mayer, Angelique Pouponneau, Cyrus Taraporevala, Samir Ibrahim, Brad Kreps, Tom Hodgman, Christina Leijonhufvud, K. Robert Turner, Dan Millman, Grant Brooke, Christopher Kip, Jens Aas, Campe Goodman, Meredith Joly, Rowan Douglas, David Hoile, Adam Gillett, Paula Pagniez, Roger Urwin, Susanne Schmitt, David MacDonald, Liz London, James Rogers, Joost Oorthuizen, Nienke Stam, and Maryanne Hancock.

Notes

1 Angelique Pouponneau, interview by the authors and research team, May 14, 2020. All subsequent quotes from Pouponneau are from the same interview.

2 Global Sustainable Investment Alliance, *2018 Global Sustainable Investment Review*, April 16, 2019, http://www.gsi-alliance.org/wp-content/uploads/2019/06/GSIR_Review2018F.pdf (accessed September 9, 2020).

3 Mathieu Benhamou, Emily Chasan, and Saijel Kishan, "The Biggest ESG Funds Are Beating the Market," *Bloomberg*, January 29, 2020, https://www.bloomberg.com/graphics/2020-ten-funds-with-a-conscience/ (accessed October 23, 2020).

4 "Annual Impact Investor Survey 2019," Global Impact Investing Network, June 19, 2019, https://thegiin.org/impact-investing/need-to-know (accessed October 23, 2020).

5 Jon Hale, "ESG Funds Setting a Record Pace for Launches in 2020," Morningstar, June 24, 2020, https://www.morningstar.com/articles/989209/esg-funds-setting-a-record-pace-for-launches-in-2020 (accessed October 23, 2020).

6 David MacDonald, interview by the authors and research team, April 30, 2020. All subsequent quotes from MacDonald are from the same interview.

7 Milton Friedman, "A Friedman Doctrine - The Social Responsibility of Business Is to Increase Its Profits," *New York Times*, September 13, 1970, https://www.nytimes.com/1970/09/13/archives/a-friedman-doctrine-the-social-responsibility-of-business-is-to.html (accessed September 9, 2020).

8 Colin Mayer, interview by the authors and research team, April 30, 2020. All subsequent quotes from Mayer are from the same interview.

9 Michael E. Porter and Mark R. Kramer, "Creating Shared Value," *Harvard Business Review*, January–February 2011, https://hbr.org/2011/01/the-big-idea-creating-shared-value (accessed September 9, 2020).

10 Lynn Stout, *The Shareholder Value Myth: How Putting Shareholders First Harms Investors, Corporations, and the Public* (San Francisco: Berrett-Koehler, 2012), https://www.bkconnection.com/books/title/the-shareholder-value-myth.

11 Liesel Pritzker Simmons, interview by the authors and research team, April 27, 2020. All subsequent quotes from Pritzker Simmons are from the same interview.

12 "Sustainable Signals," Morgan Stanley Institute for Sustainable Investing, 2019, https://www.morganstanley.com/content/dam/msdotcom/infographics

/sustainable-investing/Sustainable_Signals_Individual_Investor_White_Paper _Final.pdf (accessed October 23, 2020).

13 "The Individual Imperative: Retail Impact Investing Uncovered," Longitude, June 2019, https://www.rockefellerfoundation.org/report/individual-imperative -retail-impact-investing-uncovered/ (accessed October 23, 2020).

14 World Business Council for Sustainable Development and United Nations Environment Programme Finance Initiative, *Translating ESG into Sustainable Business Value*, March 2010, https://www.unepfi.org/fileadmin/documents /translatingESG.pdf (accessed November 19, 2020).

15 Torben Möger Pedersen, interview by the authors and research team, April 23, 2020. All subsequent quotes from Möger Pedersen are from the same interview.

16 Rowan Douglas, interview by the authors and research team, May 13, 2020. All subsequent quotes from Douglas are from the same interview.

17 "Business Roundtable Redefines the Purpose of a Corporation to Promote 'an Economy That Serves All Americans,'" Business Roundtable, August 19, 2019, https://www.businessroundtable.org/business-roundtable-redefines-the -purpose-of-a-corporation-to-promote-an-economy-that-serves-all-americans (accessed September 9, 2020).

18 "The World Economic Forum Annual Meeting 2020," World Economic Forum, January 2020, https://www.weforum.org/events/world-economic-forum-annual -meeting-2020 (accessed September 9, 2020).

19 J. Firth and M. Colley, *The Adaptation Tipping Point: Are UK Businesses Climate Proof?* (Oxford, UK: Acclimatise and UKCIP, 2006), https://www.sustain abilitywestmidlands.org.uk/wp-content/uploads/Are_UK_Businesses_Climate -proof_-_UKCIP_20061.pdf.

20 "Two-Thirds of Major UK Companies to Incorporate Climate Change Risks and Opportunities in This Year's Annual Reporting," Carbon Trust, January 23, 2019, https://www.carbontrust.com/news-and-events/news/two-thirds-of-major -uk-companies-to-incorporate-climate-change-risks-and (accessed September 9, 2020).

21 "Unlocking the Inclusive Growth Story of the 21st Century: Accelerating Climate Change in Urgent Times," New Climate Economy, September 6, 2018, https://newclimateeconomy.report/2018/ (accessed September 9, 2020).

22 "Global Social Mobility Index 2020: Why Economies Benefit from Fixing Inequality," World Economic Forum, January 19, 2020, https://www.weforum .org/reports/global-social-mobility-index-2020-why-economies-benefit-from -fixing-inequality (accessed September 9, 2020).

23 Cyrus Taraporevala, interview by the authors and research team, May 4, 2020. All subsequent quotes from Taraporevala are from the same interview.

24 David McLaughlin and Annie Masa, "The Hidden Dangers of the Great Index Fund Takeover," *Bloomberg*, January 9, 2020, https://www.bloomberg.com/news

/features/2020-01-09/the-hidden-dangers-of-the-great-index-fund-takeover
(accessed October 23, 2020).

25 Jessie Woolley-Wilson, interview by the authors and research team, June 3, 2020.
All subsequent quotes from Woolley-Wilson are from the same interview.

26 Heather Perlberg, "Carlyle Breaks from Pack, Plans Impact Investing Across
Firm," *Bloomberg*, February 26, 2020, https://www.bloomberg.com/news/articles
/2020-02-26/carlyle-breaks-from-pack-promising-impact-investing-across-firm
(accessed October 23, 2020).

27 Mikael Holter, "Norway Plans to Spend Record $41 Billion of Oil Wealth in
Crisis," *Bloomberg*, May 20, 2020, https://www.bloombergquint.com/markets
/norway-plans-to-spend-record-41-billion-of-oil-wealth-in-crisis (accessed
October 23, 2020).

28 Claudia Kruse, interview by the authors and research team, April 30, 2020. All
subsequent quotes from Kruse are from the same interview.

29 "Our Partnership for Sustainable Capital Markets," GPIF, CalSTRS, and USS,
March 2, 2020, https://www.gpif.go.jp/en/investment/Our_Partnership_for
_Sustainable_Capital_Markets_0309.pdf (accessed September 9, 2020).

30 "Brunel Pension Partnership Statement," Brunel Pension Partnership,
January 2020, https://www.brunelpensionpartnership.org/2020/01/27/30bn
-pension-partnership-calls-finance-sector-not-fit-for-purpose-for-addressing
-climate-change/ (accessed October 23, 2020).

31 Government Pension Investment Fund (GPIF), *Stewardship Activities Report
2018*, February 2019, https://www.gpif.go.jp/en/investment/gpif_stewardship
_activities_report_2018.pdf (accessed September 9, 2019).

32 "The World's Largest Pension Fund Updates on the Significant Steps It Has
Taken in Implementing Its ESG and Stewardship Strategy in Public Markets,"
The Future of Sustainable Finance, Responsible Investor Digital Festival,
June 19, 2020, https://na.eventscloud.com/website/12675/agenda/ (accessed
October 23, 2020).

33 Billy Nauman and Leo Lewis, "Moral Money Special Edition: Hiro Mizuno,
Japan's $1.6tn Man," *Financial Times*, December 12, 2019, https://www.ft.com
/content/e71a387a-1c5c-11ea-97df-cc63de1d73f4 (accessed September 9, 2020).

34 "2018 Asset Owner Survey," Bfinance, September 2018, https://www.bfinance
.com/insights/asset-owner-survey-2018/asset-owner-survey-2018-download/
(accessed September 9, 2020).

35 David Hoile, interview by the authors and research team, May 13, 2020. All
subsequent quotes from Hoile are from the same interview.

36 Morgan Stanley, Institute for Sustainable Investing, *Sustainable Signals: Growth
and Opportunity in Asset Management*, February 21, 2019, https://www
.morganstanley.com/assets/pdfs/2415532_Sustainable_Signals_Asset_Mgmt_L
.pdf (accessed September 9, 2020).

37   "Investment Strategies - Housing," Turner Impact Capital website, https:// turnerimpact.com/housing/ (accessed October 23, 2020).

38   K. Robert "Bobby" Turner, interview by the authors, May 14, 2020. All subsequent quotes from Turner are from the same interview.

39   "The World's Largest Fund Managers," Thinking Ahead Institute, October 28, 2019, https://www.thinkingaheadinstitute.org/en/Library/Public/Research-and -Ideas/2019/10/P_I_500_2019_Survey (accessed September 9, 2020).

40   "The State of Climate Tech 2020," PWC, September 2020, https://www.pwc.com/gx/ en/services/sustainability/publications/state-of-climate-tech-2020.html (accessed December 5, 2020).

41   Paul A. Gompers, Will Gornall, Steven N. Kaplan, and Ilya A. Strebulaev, "How Do Venture Capitalists Make Decisions?" (Stanford University Graduate School of Business Research Paper No. 16-33, European Corporate Governance Institute (ECGI) - Finance Working Paper No. 477/2016, August 1, 2016), https://ssrn.com/abstract=2801385 (accessed September 9, 2020).

42   Andrew Kuper, interview by the authors and research team, May 4, 2020. All subsequent quotes from Kuper are from the same interview.

43   Ken Njoroge, interview by the authors and research team, June 3, 2020. All subsequent quotes from Njoroge are from the same interview.

44   Andrew Dawber, interview by the authors and research team, June 16, 2020. All subsequent quotes from Dawber are from the same interview.

45   Nephele Kirong, "Aquila European Renewables Income Fund Raises €154.3M in IPO," S&P Global, May 31, 2019, https://www.spglobal.com/marketintelligence /en/news-insights/trending/d1gmXTB-PSu2IxfrHj20Gw2 (accessed November 25, 2020).

46   The Renewables Infrastructure Group (TRIG) website, https://www.trig-ltd.com (accessed October 23, 2020).

47   "Who We Are," Amalgamated Bank website, https://www.amalgamatedbank .com/who-we-are (accessed October 23, 2020).

48   "Global ESG Money Market Fund Dashboard: End-2019," Fitch Ratings, February 12, 2020, https://www.fitchratings.com/research/fund-asset-managers /global-esg-money-market-fund-dashboard-end-2019-12-02-2020 (accessed October 23, 2020).

49   Stephen Liberatore, interview by the authors and research team, June 10, 2020. All subsequent quotes from Liberatore are from the same interview.

50   Campe Goodman, interview by the authors and research team, June 9, 2020. All subsequent quotes from Goodman are from the same interview.

51   "Oil Crash Makes Danish Wind Power Firm the Nordics' Biggest Energy Company," Reuters, March 10, 2020, https://www.reuters.com/article/idUSL8N2B32RM (accessed November 25, 2020).

52   Nathalie Thomas, "Vestas Ends 2019 with Record Number of Orders," *Financial Times*, February 5, 2020, https://www.ft.com/content/9a33604e-480e-11ea-aeb3 -955839e06441 (accessed October 23, 2020).

53   Lizzy Gurdus, "ESG: This Is a 'Watershed Moment' for Investing in Social Advocacy, Says NAACP ETF Creator," CNBC, June 16, 2020, https://www.cnbc .com/2020/06/16/naacp-etf-creators-on-the-rise-of-esg-social-advocacy-in -investing.html (accessed October 23, 2020).

54   Maryanne Hancock, interview by the authors and research team, April 15, 2020. All subsequent quotes from Hancock are from the same interview.

55   James Mackintosh, "Is Tesla or Exxon More Sustainable? It Depends Whom You Ask," *Wall Street Journal*, September 17, 2018, https://www.wsj.com/articles/is -tesla-or-exxon-more-sustainable-it-depends-whom-you-ask-1537199931 (accessed September 9, 2020).

56   Hendrik Bartel, "Response to WSJ Article: Is Tesla or Exxon More Sustainable?," Truvalue Labs, September 27, 2018, https://www.truvaluelabs.com/blog/truvalue -labs-response-to-wsj-article-is-tesla-or-exxon-more-sustainable (accessed September 9, 2020).

57   Florian Berg, Julian F. Kölbel, and Roberto Rigobon, "Aggregate Confusion: The Divergence of ESG Ratings" (MIT Sloan School Working Paper 5822-19, May 17, 2020), https://ssrn.com/abstract=3438533 (accessed September 9, 2020).

58   Andres Portilla, Sonja Gibbs, and Katie Rismanchi, "Sustainable Finance Policy & Regulation: The Case for Greater International Alignment" (Institute of International Finance, March 2020), https://www.iif.com/Portals/0/Files/content /Regulatory/IIFStaffPaper-Sustainable%20Finance%20Case%20for%20 Greater%20International%20Alignment-2020%2003%2002-Final.pdf (accessed September 9, 2020), p. 9.

59   "Promoting Clarity and Compatibility in the Sustainability Landscape," Sustainability Accounting Standards Board and Global Reporting Initiative, July 13, 2020, https://www.sasb.org/wp-content/uploads/2020/07/GRI-SASB -joint-statement_2020_07_13_FINAL.pdf (accessed October 23, 2020).

60   "Rate the Raters 2020: Investor Survey and Interview Results," SustainAbility, March 2020, https://sustainability.com/wp-content/uploads/2020/03 /sustainability-ratetheraters2020-report.pdf (accessed September 9, 2020).

61   BNP Paribas, *Great Expectations for ESG: What Is Next for Asset Owners and Managers*, 2017, https://securities.bnpparibas.com/files/live/sites/web/files /private/surv_esg_en_2017-07-07.pdf (accessed November 20, 2020), p. 18.

62   "Sustainability Accounting Standards Board (SASB) Industry Standards," SASB, 2020, https://www.sasb.org/standards-overview/ (accessed September 9, 2020).

63   "Case Study: Caisse des Dépôts," UN Principles for Responsible Investment (UNPRI), January 31, 2019, https://www.unpri.org/credit-ratings/credit-risk -case-study-caisse-des-depots-/4027.article (accessed September 9, 2020).

64   Global Impact Investing Network, *The State of Impact Management and Measurement Practice*, 2nd ed., January 2020, https://thegiin.org/assets/GIIN _State%20of%20Impact%20Measurement%20and%20Management%20Practice _Second%20Edition.pdf (accessed September 9, 2020).

65   Amanda Albright and Mallika Mitra, "Satellites Are Helping the Municipal Bond Market Assess Climate Risk," *Bloomberg*, February 6, 2020, https://www .bloomberg.com/news/articles/2020-02-06/satellites-are-helping-the-municipal -bond-market-assess-climate-risk (accessed September 9, 2020).

66   Christina Leijonhufvud, interview by the authors and research team, June 11, 2020. All subsequent quotes from Leijonhufvud are from the same interview.

67   "Investing for Impact: Operating Principles for Impact Management," International Finance Corporation (IFC), February 2019, https://www .impactprinciples.org/principles (accessed September 9, 2020).

68   Hans Peter Lankes, interview by the authors and research team, April 27, 2020. All subsequent quotes from Lankes are from the same interview.

69   Tideline, *Making the Mark: Investor Alignment with the Operating Principles for Impact Management*, April 2020, http://tideline.com/wp-content/uploads /Tideline_Report_Making_the_Mark_April_2020.pdf (accessed September 9, 2020).

70   Susanne Schmitt, interview by the authors and research team, May 21, 2020. All subsequent quotes from Schmitt are from the same interview.

71   Sarah Murray and Conrad Heine, *Dangerous Liaisons: How Businesses Are Learning to Work with Their New Stakeholders*, Economist Intelligence Unit, 2010, http://graphics.eiu.com/upload/eb/EIU_New_stakeholders_Final_WEB .pdf (accessed September 9, 2020).

72   Mark Florman, Martim Jacinto Facada, and Robyn Klingler-Vidra, "A Critical Evaluation of Social Impact Assessment Methodologies and a Call to Measure Economic and Social Impact Holistically Through the External Rate of Return Platform" (LSE Enterprise Working Paper No. 1602, February 2016), http:// eprints.lse.ac.uk/65393/1/Assessing%20social%20impact%20assessment%20 methods%20report%20-%20final.pdf (accessed September 9, 2020).

73   "DreamBox Learning," CrunchBase, July 2020, https://www.crunchbase.com /organization/dreambox-learning#section-funding-rounds (accessed October 23, 2020).

74   Susanna Rust, "APG, PGGM Set Out Investment Routes to UN Development Goals," *Investment and Pensions Europe*, July 5, 2017, https://www.ipe.com/apg -pggm-set-out-investment-routes-to-un-development-goals-/10019777.article (accessed October 23, 2020).

75   Georgia Levenson Keohane and Saadia Madsbjerg, "The Innovative Finance Revolution: Private Capital for the Public Good," *Foreign Affairs*, July/August 2016, https://www.foreignaffairs.com/articles/2016-06-05/innovative-finance-revolution (accessed September 9, 2020).

76 Charlotte Kaiser, interview by the authors and research team, April 27, 2020. All subsequent quotes from Kaiser are from the same interview.

77 "CCRIF Reaches US$100 Million Milestone in Payouts," CCRIF, September 19, 2007, https://www.ccrif.org/node/11915 (accessed October 23, 2020).

78 Philippe Zaouati, interview by the authors and research team, May 14, 2020. All subsequent quotes from Zaouati are from the same interview.

79 Quoted in Caroline Preston, "Getting Back More Than a Warm Feeling," *New York Times*, November 8, 2012, https://www.nytimes.com/2012/11/09/giving /investors-profit-by-giving-through-social-impact-bonds.html (accessed September 9, 2020).

80 Blue Forest Conservation, *The Forest Resilience Bond: Annual Impact Report 2019*, 2019, https://static1.squarespace.com/static/556a1885e4b0bdc6f0794659/t /5ec6db4f9f34555fcdee75c2/1590090595470/FRB+Impact+Report+2019.pdf (accessed September 9, 2020).

81 Environmental Defense Fund, *An Investor's Guide to Methane: Engaging with Oil and Gas Companies to Manage a Rising Risk*, October 2016, https://www.edf .org/sites/default/files/content/investor_guide_final.pdf (accessed September 9, 2020).

82 David Blood, interview by the authors and research team, May 11, 2020. All subsequent quotes from Blood are from the same interview.

83 James Fallows, "The Planet-Saving, Capitalism-Subverting, Surprisingly Lucrative Investment Secrets of Al Gore," *The Atlantic*, November 2015, https://www.theatlantic.com/magazine/archive/2015/11/the-planet-saving -capitalism-subverting-surprisingly-lucrative-investment-secrets-of-al-gore /407857/ (accessed September 9, 2020).

84 "Renewed Sustainable Finance Strategy and Implementation of the Action Plan on Financing Sustainable Growth," European Commission, updated August 5, 2020, https://ec.europa.eu/info/publications/180308-action-plan-sustainable -growth_en (accessed September 9, 2020).

85 "EU Taxonomy Alignment Case Studies," UN Principles for Responsible Investment (PRI), September 9, 2020, https://www.unpri.org/eu-taxonomy -alignment-case-studies/testing-the-taxonomy-insights-from-the-pri-taxonomy -practitioners-group/6409.article (accessed September 10, 2020).

86 Transcript of speech delivered by Nikhil Rathi, Chief Executive of Financial Conduct Authority, at an online conference hosted by the City of London, November 2020, https://custom.cvent.com/8644FD66069649369747A352DBAB0 7C3/files/1e02ebd039574d398f52acea304abcc8.pdf (accessed November 10, 2020).

87 "Recommendation from the Investor-as-Owner Subcommittee of the SEC Investor Advisory Committee Relating to ESG Disclosure," Securities and Exchange Commission, May 2020, https://www.sec.gov/spotlight/investor -advisory-committee-2012/recommendation-of-the-investor-as-owner -subcommittee-on-esg-disclosure.pdf (accessed September 9, 2020).

88 "Financial Factors in Selecting Plan Investments," 85 FR 72846, November 13, 2020, https://www.federalregister.gov/documents/2020/11/13/2020-24515/ financial-factors-in-selecting-plan-investments (accessed December 5, 2020).

89 "Task Force on Climate-Related Financial Disclosures Pilot Projects," UNEP Finance Initiative, https://www.unepfi.org/climate-change/tcfd/ (accessed September 9, 2020).

90 UNEP Finance Initiative, *Changing Course: A Comprehensive Investor Guide to Scenario-Based Methods for Climate Risk Assessment, in Response to the TCFD,* May 2019, https://www.unepfi.org/wordpress/wp-content/uploads/2019/05 /TCFD-Changing-Course-Oct-19.pdf (accessed September 9, 2020), p. 5.

91 "The ESG Lens on COVID-19, Part 1," S&P Global Ratings, April 20, 2020, https://www.spglobal.com/ratings/en/research/articles/200420-the-esg-lens-on -covid-19-part-1-11444298 (accessed September 9, 2020).

92 Brian Deese, Philipp Hildebrand, Richard Kushel, and Ashley Schulten, *Sustainability: The Bond That Endures; Tools and Insights for ESG Investing in Fixed Income,* BlackRock Investment Institute, November 2019, https://www .blackrock.com/corporate/literature/whitepaper/bii-sustainable-investing -bonds-november-2019.pdf (accessed September 9, 2020).

93 Michael Jelinske, interview by the authors and research team, May 22, 2020. All subsequent quotes from Jelinske are from the same interview.

94 Amaan Nizaar Khalfan, interview by the authors and research team, May 28, 2020. All subsequent quotes from Khalfan are from the same interview.

95 Subodh Mishra, "An Overview of U.S. Shareholder Proposal Filings," Harvard Law School Forum on Corporate Governance, February 28, 2018, https:// corpgov.law.harvard.edu/2018/02/28/an-overview-of-u-s-shareholder-proposal -filings/ (accessed September 9, 2020).

96 Rob Berridge and Natasha Nurjadin, "Why Do Some Large Asset Managers Still Vote Against Most Climate-Related Shareholder Proposals?," Ceres, March 13, 2020, https://www.ceres.org/news-center/blog/why-do-some-large-asset -managers-still-vote-against-most-climate-related (accessed September 9, 2020).

97 "Leadership for the Decade of Action," Russell Reynolds Associates, June 2020, https://www.russellreynolds.com/insights/thought-leadership/sustainability-a -leadership-imperative (accessed September 9, 2020).

98 Soohun Kim and Aaron Yoon, "Analyzing Active Managers' Commitment to ESG: Evidence from United Nations Principles for Responsible Investment" (Korea Advanced Institute of Science and Technology and Northwestern University, March 17, 2020), https://ssrn.com/abstract=3555984 (accessed September 9, 2020).

99 Frédéric Samama, interview by the authors and research team, May 9, 2020. All subsequent quotes from Samama are from the same interview.

100 Brad Kreps, interview by the authors and research team, June 4, 2020. All subsequent quotes from Kreps are from the same interview.

101 Grant Brooke, interview by the authors and research team, June 4, 2020. All subsequent quotes from Brooke are from the same interview.

102 Samir Ibrahim, interview by the authors and research team, June 1, 2020. All subsequent quotes from Ibrahim are from the same interview.

103 Roger Urwin, interview by the authors and research team, May 28, 2020. All subsequent quotes from Urwin are from the same interview.

104 Kenneth Lay, interview by the authors and research team, May 13, 2020. All subsequent quotes from Lay are from the same interview.

105 "Survey on Compensation Structure (Incentive Scheme) of GPIF Asset Managers," Government Pension Investment Fund (GPIF), July 8, 2019, https://www.gpif.go.jp/en/investment/stewardship/survey.html (accessed September 9, 2020).

106 Florence Chong, "Government Pension Investment Fund: Widening the Reach," Investment and Pensions Europe (IPE), October 2019, https://www.ipe.com /government-pension-investment-fund-widening-the-reach/10033547.article (accessed September 9, 2020).

107 Norges Bank Investment Management, *Network on Children's Rights in the Garment and Footwear Sector: Summary Report 2017–2019*, June 2020, https:// www.unicef.org/media/70126/file/Network-on-childrens-rights-in-the-garment -and-footwear-sector-summary-2020.pdf (accessed September 9, 2020), p. 1.

108 Attracta Mooney, "BlackRock Accused of Climate Change Hypocrisy," *Financial Times*, May 17, 2020, https://www.ft.com/content/0e489444-2783-4f6e-a006 -aa8126d2ff46 (accessed September 9, 2020).

109 Terje Osmundsen, "What Does It Take to Eliminate Energy Poverty in Africa?," Power for All, December 9, 2019, https://www.powerforall.org/insights/africa /what-does-it-take-eliminate-energy-poverty-africa (accessed November 25, 2020).

110 "Our Story," Portfolia website, https://www.portfolia.co/our-story (accessed November 20, 2020).

111 World Economic Forum, *Nature Risk Rising: Why the Crisis Engulfing Nature Matters for Business and the Economy*, January 2020, http://www3.weforum.org /docs/WEF_New_Nature_Economy_Report_2020.pdf (accessed September 9, 2020).

112 Bettina Reinboth and Nikolaj Halkjaer Pedersen, "A Shield Against COVID-19: Embedding Human Rights in Investment," UNPRI, May 1, 2020, https://www .unpri.org/pri-blogs/a-shield-against-covid-19-embedding-human-rights-in -investment/5732.article (accessed September 9, 2020).

113 "Leadership for the Decade of Action," Russell Reynolds Associates.

Index

About the Authors

As funders, investors, and conveners who have partnered with every sector and worked in every corner of the globe to create and grow the practice of sustainable and impact investing, authors Judith Rodin and Saadia Madsbjerg have a unique perspective of the enormous market opportunity as well as the challenges facing the industry.

Judith Rodin is former president of the University of Pennsylvania and of The Rockefeller Foundation, one of the world's leading philanthropies. As Rockefeller's president, she positioned the 101-year-old institution to influence decision-makers, to be a catalyst for innovation, and to develop cross-sector solutions that could address the challenges facing the planet and its people in the twenty-first century. She and her colleagues helped coin the term "impact investing" and spent millions of dollars in philanthropic capital to build critical infrastructure for this, then developing, field. She has also served on the boards of nine public companies and currently serves on the boards of several venture-capital-backed companies.

Saadia Madsbjerg is a former managing director of The Rockefeller Foundation. She led the foundation's financial innovation program to seed-fund the development and launch of new financial instruments designed to channel money from the capital markets toward sustainable development. She has also served as a trusted advisor to Fortune 500 companies on corporate strategy.

About Wharton School Press

Wharton School Press, the book publishing arm of the Wharton School of the University of Pennsylvania, was established to inspire bold, insightful thinking within the global business community.

Wharton School Press publishes a select list of award-winning, best-selling, and thought-leading books that offer trusted business knowledge to help leaders at all levels meet the challenges of today and the opportunities of tomorrow. Led by a spirit of innovation and experimentation, Wharton School Press leverages groundbreaking digital technologies and has pioneered a fast-reading business book format that fits readers' busy lives, allowing them to swiftly emerge with the tools and information needed to make an impact. Wharton School Press books offer guidance and inspiration on a variety of topics, including leadership, management, strategy, innovation, entrepreneurship, finance, marketing, social impact, public policy, and more.

Wharton School Press also operates an online bookstore featuring a curated selection of influential books by Wharton School faculty and Press authors published by a wide range of leading publishers.

To find books that will inspire and empower you to increase your impact and expand your personal and professional horizons, visit *wsp.wharton.upenn.edu.*

About the Wharton School

Founded in 1881 as the world's first collegiate business school, the Wharton School of the University of Pennsylvania is shaping the future of business by incubating ideas, driving insights, and creating leaders who change the world. With a faculty of more than 235 renowned professors, Wharton has 5,000 undergraduate, MBA, executive MBA, and doctoral students. Each year 13,000 professionals from around the world advance their careers through Wharton Executive Education's individual, company-customized, and online programs. More than 99,000 Wharton alumni form a powerful global network of leaders who transform business every day.

www.wharton.upenn.edu